KILCASH

A History, 1190-1801

JOHN FLOOD
PHIL FLOOD

GEOGRAPHY PUBLICATIONS

Aerial photograph of Kilcash Church and Graveyard (July 1970).
A: Kilcash castle; B: Old Kilcash churchyard; C: Oven; D: Walled gardens; E: Possible landscaping for gardens.

Published in Ireland by
Geography Publications,
Kennington Road,
Templeogue, Dublin 6W

© John Flood, Phil Flood 1999

ISBN 0 906602 66 1

Contents

Preface — iv
Table of Illustrations — vi
Timeline — viii
Introduction — x

Chapter 1: The Physical Remains — 1
   The Church — 1
   Mausoleum — 4
   Graveyard — 7
   The Castle — 8
   The Tower Exterior — 9
   The Tower Interior — 13
   The House — 17
   Other Buildings — 22

Chapter 2: The Early History of Kilcash — 27
   Old Kilcash: The Beginnings — 27
   The de Valles of Kilcash and Dame Alice Kyteller — 31
   The Church in Kilcash before the Protestant Reformation — 36
   The Butlers and Kilcash: Early Connections — 36
   The Butlers of Kilcash — 37
   Walter Butler of Kilcash (1559?-1632/3) — 39
   Richard Butler of Kilcash (c. 1616-1701) — 42
   The Church in Kilcash between the Reformation and the Eighteenth Century — 47

Chapter 3: The Eighteenth Century — 59
   Thomas Butler (d. 1738) and Margaret Burke, Viscountess Iveagh (d. 1744) — 59
   The Church in Kilcash in the Eighteenth Century — 69
   John Butler of Kilcash (d. 1766) — 70
   1766-1795: The Fall of Kilcash — 73

Chapter 3: The Literary Heritage — 85
   'Cill Chaise' — 85
   Other Compositions Associated with Kilcash — 95

Appendix 1: Burials in Cemetery — 109
Appendix 2: Headstone Inscriptions — 114
Appendix 3: *Cill Chaise* – Textual Notes — 119
Appendix 4: *Cúirt an ghrinn seo Ormond* – Textual Notes — 123
Genealogy of the Butlers of Kilcash — 125
Bibliography — 126

Preface

In Ireland Kilcash is probably best known for the Irish song *Cill Chaise* (sometimes called *A Lament for Kilcash*). The song, however, only glances at a small and relatively recent part of the history that underlies the ruins which can be seen there today. We have lived, so to speak, in the shadow of that church and tower and *Cill Chaise* was taught to us in national school. Having spent years wandering around Old Kilcash and having come across snippets of its history and the associated folklore we wanted to look somewhat further than the relatively cursory treatments of the place which appear as footnotes in larger histories. The end result is this book which we hope will be an accessible starting point for an exploration of the archaeology and history of Old Kilcash.

The first chapter of this book, on the archaeology of Kilcash, is greatly endebted to our exploration and discussion of the site with Mr Con Manning (Dúchas) and Ms Jean Farrelly (Archaeological Survey of Tipperary), both of whom were kind enough to read our drafts of the relevant material in addition to visiting the ruins.

Chapter IV, on the literary heritage of Kilcash, owes a good deal to the efforts of others. Prof. Dáithí Ó hÓgáin (UCD) produced an edition of the Irish text and of *Cill Chaise* accompanied by an English prose translation, while the poet Ms Eiléan Ní Chuilleanáin (TCD) wrote a poetic translation based on Prof. Ó hÓgáin's Irish text. Dr Tadhg Ó Dúshláine (NUIM) provided us with a modern Irish edition and English prose translation of the poem *The Lady Iveagh*. Finally, Dr Pádraig Ó Macháin (Dublin Institute for Advanced Studies) drew our attention to the Irish poem *This Pleasure-Court of Ormond* which he subsequently edited and translated.

We owe particular thanks to our indefatigable photographer Mr John Foley, as well as to Dr Ray Gillespie (NUIM), and Dr William Nolan (UCD) both of whom read early drafts of parts of the text. We also gratefully acknowledge the financial support for this publication which came from the Heritage Council under the 1999 Publications' Grant Scheme.

We benefited enormously from the practical help, encouragement and advice of a great number of people without whose aid our research would have been well-nigh impossible, these include Mr Gerard Bourke (Dúchas), Mr Garvin Casey, Prof. R. V. Comerford (NUIM), Rev. Dr Adrian Empey, Ms Caitríona Gibbs, Messrs. Jack and

Michael Kehoe, Ms Beatrice Kelly (Heritage Council), Br Robert Molloy (Franciscan Friary, Clonmel), Mr Joe Norton (Dúchas), Colonel Donal O'Carroll, Mr Pádraig Ó Cearbhaill (Ordnance Survey), Rev. Christy O'Dwyer (St Patrick's College, Thurles), Dr Éamonn Ó hÓgáin (RIA), Mrs Ann O'Reilly, Colonel Eoghan Ó Néill, Mrs Una Power, Mr P. D. Sweetman (Dúchas), Mrs Ita Tobin and Dr Bernadette Williams (TCD).

Finally, our research would have been impossible without the assistance and good-will of the Council of Trustees and the staff of the National Library, the National Library Manuscripts Reading Room (particularly Mr Tom Desmond and Dr Noel Kissane), the Library and the Manuscripts Department of Trinity College Dublin, the Irish Traditional Music Archive (Ms Róisín Ní Bhriain and Mr Nicholas Carolan), The Courtauld Institute, London (Ms Melanie Blake), Kilkenny Castle, the County Library, Thurles (Ms Mary Guinan-Darmody), The Registry of Deeds and the Library of the Royal Irish Academy (Ms Bernadette Cunningham).

Needless to say, whatever faults or omissions remain in the text are entirely our own responsibility. If anyone notices any errors or knows of any additional information about Kilcash we would be very grateful to hear about it.

John Flood
Phil Flood
Kilcash, Co. Tipperary
1999

Note on Conventions:
A list of the abbreviations used in the endnotes appears in the bibliography under 'Manuscript Sources'. We have retained abbreviations and unusual or variant orthography (with the exception of superscriptions) in all quotation from primary material. As the books follows a chronological sequence it was considered unnecessary to provide an index. Reference to particular people or events can readily be found with the aid of the Timeline and the Butler family tree.

Table of Illustrations

Cover
Front: Kilcash Castle viewed from the South (Ita Tobin)

Plates
Frontispiece: *Aerial photograph of Old Kilcash* (Cambridge University Collection of Air Photographs: copyright reserved)
Plate 1: *Missing archway between nave & chancel* (John Foley)
Plate 2: *Round headed windows: view of north window through south window* (John Foley)
Plate 3: *Romanesque church doorway in south wall* (John Foley)
Plate 4: *Mausoleum, south wall* (John Foley)
Plate 5: *Detail from headstone of "Kilmurry School"* (John Foley)
Plate 6: *Worn grave slab with passion symbols* (John Foley)
Plate 7: *Kilcash Castle from the north west* (John Foley)
Plate 8: *Entrance doorway to castle* (John Foley)
Plates 9a & b: *West wall – machicolation above door & chimneys* (John Foley)
Plate 10: *Corner machicolation – north east* (John Foley)
Plate 11: *View of castle from south east* (John Foley)
Plate 12: *Murder hole* (John Foley)
Plate 13: *Doorway off stairs* (John Foley)
Plate 14: *Inside of north wall viewed from the south* (John Flood)
Plate 15: *Interior of tower* (John Foley)
Plate 16: *South wall of house and tower* (John Foley)
Plate 17: *The oven, to the east of the tower* (John Foley)
Plate 18: *Standing gable of outbuilding viewed from north east* (John Foley)
Plate 19: *Standing gable of outbuilding viewed from south west* (John Foley)
Plate 20: *Thomas Butler of Kilcash* (Courtauld Institute of Art)
Plate 21: *Archbishop Christopher Butler* (Courtauld Institute of Art)
Plate 22: *Margaret, Viscountess Iveagh* (Photograph: James Maher ed. 1954. Signature: NLI Ormonde Papers MS. 2478/251)
Plate 23: *Inventory of kitchen of Kilcash Castle, 1753* (NLI Ormond Papers MS. 2621/231)
Plate 24: *Walter Butler, 16th Earl of Ormonde* (Courtauld Institute of Art)
Plate 25: *Anne Wandesford* (Courtauld Institute of Art)
Plate 26: *Walter Butler, 18th Earl of Ormonde* (Courtauld Institute of Art)

Plate 27: *Opening verses of Cill Chaise from John O'Daly's manuscript* (RIA MS. 12 E 24)

Illustrations

Illustration 1: *Dimensions of the castle ruins*
Illustration 2: *A drawing of Kilcash Castle in 1851* (UCDF, Fogarty's Ms. Antiquites [sic] of Iverk Co. Kilkenny)
Illustration 3: *A map of 1777 showing the Butler houses at Kilcash and Garryricken*
Illustration 4: *Plan of the cemetery*

Acknowledgements: We are grateful to the following institutions for permission to reproduce plates: Kilkenny Castle (plates 20, 21, 24, 25, 26); the Council and Trustees of the National Library of Ireland (plates 22, 23); the Royal Irish Academy (plate 27), the Department of Irish Folklore, UCD (Illustration 2).

Timeline

c. 550   Possible monastic foundation of Colman Mac Erc at Kilcash.

846   Death of Diarmuid of Kilcash.

c. 1200   Baldwin Niger grants church of Kilcash to the Hospital of St John the Baptist in Dublin.

c. 1300   Richard de Valle, tenant of Kilcash.

1324   Trial of Alice Kyteler, formerly wife of Richard de Valle.

1478   Statues of Kilcash.

c. 1540   Kilcash passes to the Earl of Ormond.

1545   Earl of Ormond leaves Kilcash to his son, John Butler.

1563   John Butler wounded in battle with Geraldines. Dies in 1564 or 1670.

1642-51   English Civil War.

1603   Death of Queen Elizabeth. Accession of James I.

1614   Walter Butler of Kilcash, John Butler's son, becomes 11th Earl of Ormond.

1619   Thomas, Walter's son drowns.

1625   James I of England dies. Charles I crowned king.

1632-3   Walter dies. Kilcash passes to his grandson, Richard.

1641   Rising in Ulster.

1642   Catholic Confederation formed at Kilkenny.

1649   Charles I executed.

1650   Clonmel surrenders to Cromwell's army.

1660   Restoration of the Monarchy in England.

1661   James, grandson of Walter Butler, created 1st Duke of Ormonde.

1685	Charles II dies. James II crowned.
1688	'The Glorious Revolution'. William and Mary proclaimed by English Parliament.
1691	Jacobites lose battle at Aughrim. Thomas Butler of Kilcash captured.
1700	Walter Butler of Garryricken – Richard Butler of Kilcash's son – dies.
1701	Death of Richard Butler. Kilcash passes to his grandson, Thomas.
1712	Christopher Butler, Thomas of Kilcash's brother, consecrated Archbishop of Cashel.
1738	Col. Thomas Butler of Kilcash dies.
1739	John, son of Thomas Butler and Lady Iveagh, converts to Anglicanism.
1744	Lady Iveagh dies.
1760	John Butler of Kilcash becomes de jure 15th Earl of Ormonde.
1766	John Butler dies without an heir. Kilcash passes to his cousin Walter Butler of Garryricken, de jure 16th Earl of Ormonde.
1783	Walter Butler dies. Kilcash passes to his son, John Butler (Jack o' the Castle), recognised as 17th Earl of Ormonde by Irish Parliament.
1795	Jack o' the Castle dies. Kilcash passes to his son, Walter, 18th Earl of Ormonde.
c. 1800	Materials of Kilcash castle sold to James Power, merchant.
1922	General Prout shells castle.
1998	Castle passes into the possession of the State from the Ormonde Estate.

Introduction

This book introduces some of the history of 'Old' Kilcash in South Tipperary.[1] It is known locally as 'Old' Kilcash because the modern village of Kilcash is two kilometres away, higher up on the south foot of Slievenamon.[2]

We begin, in Chapter I, with a description of the archaeological features of the ruins of the church and the castle. An archaeological excavation of the castle remains to be carried out, however, our summary provides the visitor with a guide to the monuments as well as acting as a record of the current state of a site which is in danger of further deterioration.[3] For those who do not have the opportunity to visit the area, photographs of some of the archaeological features are included. Furthermore we have also recorded – in the appendices – the inscriptions of the gravestones in the old cemetery.

Chapter II addresses the early history of Kilcash beginning with the ecclesiastical settlement of the area and progressing through the history of the manor and its associated personalities. This history is continued in Chapter III which deals with the eighteenth century, just as Thomas Butler succeeds to Kilcash. Our study ends at the close of this century with the abandonment and subsequent ruin of the castle. After 1800 the locality is firmly centred on the current village and work remains to be done on the history of the Kilcash area in the nineteenth and twentieth centuries.[4]

Finally, with the co-operation of Professor Dáithí Ó hÓgáin and the poet Eiléan Ní Chuilleanáin, we have provided newly edited versions of the text of *Cill Chaise* in both Irish and English. Currently the song exists in several published versions of differing lengths and we felt that a new scholarly text based on the extant nineteenth century sources was called for. *Cill Chaise* and some of the lesser known poems associated with the castle are an important part of the place's later oral history and we could hardly attempt a history of its inhabitants without looking carefully at the literary as well as the historical and archaeological remains.

The Current Ownership of Kilcash
One of the most striking features of Kilcash's modern history is the high regard in which the Butler family (the last private owners of the castle) are still held in the area. The Butlers, despite the fact that they were the local landlords, are remembered in to-day's popular lore as

having been sympathetic towards their tenants. In part this may have been because of the strong connections that the Butlers had with the Catholic religion while in part it may recall the actual generosity which some members of the family showed to the tenantry. In any event, there is still a link to the Butler past as the Butler family rally is regularly welcomed in the modern village during their quadrennial Irish gatherings.

Since its ruin Old Kilcash remained in the possession of the Ormonde estate. However, under the impression that the church grounds had passed into its care under the Irish Church Act of 1869, Tipperary S. R. County Council paid for the maintenance of the graveyard and supervised work carried out in the 1980s to prevent the further deterioration of the church.

In 1973, R. B. Haughton, the agent of the Ormonde estate, wrote to what was then the Office of Public Works (OPW) to indicate that the Marquess of Ormonde would hardly refuse any offer by the State to take over possession of Old Kilcash.[5] The OPW looked into the condition of the castle, at which time it was estimated that it would require £20,000 for immediate repairs with £100 per year for its continued maintenance.[6] This sum was not available at the time and so – despite pressure from Tipperary S. R. County Council – the OPW did not think that it could responsibly undertake the care of the site.

Finally, in January 1992, after much correspondence on the matter, the OPW considered that it was in a position to take over Old Kilcash. R. B. Haughton was contacted to see if his offer of 1973 still stood. This official request on the part of the OPW was deemed acceptable by Haughton and the Ormonde estate and the OPW applied to the Department of Finance for the relevant funding.[7] Considering the bad condition of the castle there was some hesitation on the part of the Department of Finance and the issue became bogged down once more.

In the mid 1990s, in response to local pressures, the question of the fate of Old Kilcash was raised by politicians of various parties, both in the Dáil and in private correspondence with the OPW. This time there was a delay on the part of the Ormonde trustees who did not feel empowered to give away the sites, feeling it beholden on them to maximise the revenue from any sale for the benefit of the Ormonde estate. However, a sum was eventually agreed on and in February 1997 the Ormonde trustees indicated their assent.[8]

In 1997 the indenture for the transfer of 'the property known as Kilcash Castle together with the graveyard situate at Kilcash in the County of Tipperary'[9] was drawn up. For £500, the State, in the person of Síle de Valera, Minister of Arts, Heritage, Gaeltacht and the Islands purchased Old Kilcash from the Ormonde Estate which was represented by its trustees (variously from Belgium, England and the U.S.A.). Sadly, as soon as the castle passed into the possession of the Irish people its gates had to be locked and the hazardous tower closed off. However, it is hoped that work will be ongoing on the building and its environs in the next few years. It is planned that weaknesses in the structure of the tower will be repaired so that it will no longer be in danger of collapsing. Because of the precarious state of the tower and of the adjoining house wall, such repairs are a matter of some urgency (already, since we began our research, the gable of one of the outbuildings has collapsed in a storm.) Though the castle will not be restored, it is hoped that eventually the grounds can once again be opened to the public who will then be able to safely stroll around walks which have witnessed so much of the country's history.

References
1. Ordnance Survey sheet 18 (S 32 28). Old Kilcash is 91m (300 feet) above sea level.
2. Through the years the size of the civil parish seem to have changed somewhat. In the *Civil Survey* of 1640 the parish is said to be 1,421 plantation acres (2,302 statute acres) while in the 19th century it is just over 1,115 acres in area. [See R. C. Simington (1931), 272 and *Census of Ireland* (1861), 553].
3. In this volume we were unable to include the hundred or so photographs of the site which were taken by John Foley in the process of our attempting to preserve some permanent record of the place. To this end we are lodging these photographs and a catalogue in the National Photographic Archive attached to the National Library of Ireland.
4. As an extensive collection of nineteenth century rentals for the Ormond estates (including that of Kilcash) survives in the National Library of Ireland there is ample material for a study of the later history of the area.
5. Dúchas MS. Letter from R. B. Haughton from the Castle Office Kilkenny to the OPW, dated 9/7/98.
6. Dúchas MS. Report of Aighleann Ní Fhlathartaigh To OPW, 17/9/75.
7. Dúchas MS. Letter from G. Bourke, OPW to Agent of the Marquess at the Castle Office, Kilkenny, dated 16/1/92. Letter from Robert B. Houghton to G. Bourke, OPW, dated 28/1/92.
8. Dúchas MS. Record of telephone call from R. B. Haughton to Gerard Bourke of the OPW.
9. Dúchas MS.

Chapter I

The Physical Remains[1]

The Church and Graveyard
The graveyard at Old Kilcash is situated on a level piece of land on the southern slopes of Slievenamon.[2] In the north west corner of the graveyard nestle the standing remains of the old church consisting of a chancel and a later nave.* It appears that the condition of the monument has altered little during the last 150 years.[3] Beyond the church ruin, in the north east corner, stands a mausoleum used by the Butler family from the nearby castle.

The Church
The chancel, constructed mainly of local sandstone, is the earlier of the two sections and little of it now remains. The upper portion of the north wall was rebuilt and capped as a boundary wall in modern times. In the process of rebuilding a carved Romanesque stone was incorporated into this wall[4] which also bears indications that the church originally had antae (the projections of side walls beyond the building's gables: these were features of early Irish churches).[5] The east gable is almost completely destroyed with only bare evidence of a window. The south wall has had repair work carried out during County Council renovation. The wall was leaning outwards, possibly due to weak foundations and lack of adequate bonding. What was once the chancel arch – and perhaps the position of an earlier, narrower doorway[6] – is now missing and the archway is squared off to support the masonry of its gable [Plate 1]. Suggested dates for the chancel range from the tenth to the early twelfth century.[7]

The nave is somewhat higher and wider than the chancel. A different type of masonry was used, with smaller, uneven stones. This resulted in poor bonding, a feature which is clearly visible today. The north wall of the nave has a large breach near the west end and a small round-headed slit window close to the east corner. This window would

---

*The chancel (from Latin *cancelli*, the plural of 'lattice') is the part of the church which houses the sanctuary and altar. It was usually separated from the nave (the body of the church where the congregation gathered) by a decorated screen.

Plate 1:   Missing archway between nave and chancel (viewed from the chancel side).

have had an external wooden shutter the spaces for the iron fittings of which can still be seen on the exterior of the window. The west gable, with its round-headed lancet window was dismantled and rebuilt during recent conservation work. Similar to the south wall of the chancel, this wall was leaning outwards and was in a dangerous condition.[8] The south wall has a round-headed window near the east end, directly opposite the one in the north wall [Plate 2].

The principal feature of the ruin is in the south wall in the form of a badly weathered Romanesque doorway.* The doorway has three orders (or 'rows') of sandstone blocks and is relatively plain, though some of the orders exhibit the chevron pattern which is typical of Romanesque decoration† [Plate 3]. Due to the use of sandstone, the dressings of the windows and of the doorway are very eroded, though if one looks closely the remains of the doorway's original carving and decoration are in places still visible. On the inside, on the West side of the doorway, the holes for the door hinges can still be seen. Sweetman points out that Romanesque doorways are usually found in the gable-end of the nave and suggests the possibility of its current position in the south wall indicating that it was reconstructed as part of a later parish church.[9] However, this was not invariably the case and, for example, the doorway of the old church in nearby Kilsheelan or that in Cormac's Chapel in Cashel are in a similar position.

Suggested dates for the nave range from the second quarter of the twelfth century to the third quarter of the twelfth century.[10] Both chancel and nave have been disturbed by modern burials.

Any repair and conservation work referred to was carried out in the late 1980s by Tipperary (S. R.) Co. Council. The work was done with National Lottery funding, a fact indicated by the plaque on the outside of the west gable. A preliminary report recommending the repairs and reconstruction was carried out for the Co. Council in 1983 by Patrick Holland (then attached to Museum Services, Clonmel).

Acting on Patrick Holland's advice,[11] the OPW undertook limited archaeological excavation work, under the direction of its archaeologist P. D. Sweetman, in 1984. This work was carried out in the interior of the ruin. Little of significance was found in the excavation. Five pieces of carved medieval stone were recovered in the south east portion of the chancel, just under floor level. The clerk of works, Mr Feely, thought that these may have belonged to a medieval tomb.[12] Three shards of Ham Green‡ pottery were found in the disturbed ground of

---

*'Romanesque' refers to architecture based to some degree on Roman art. In Ireland it is associated with the twelfth century. Individual national characteristics mark the Romanesque buildings which are to be found across Europe which contributes to the controversy surrounding their dating. [See H. G. Leask (1977), 79-81].

†The chevron is the zigzag (incised or in relief) of blocks which can be seen at the top of the archway. [See H. G. Leask (1977), 95].

‡Ham Green pottery is frequently found in Ireland. It is so called as it originated from the kilns at Ham Green near Bristol in England, which were major trading partners with Anglo-Norman Ireland. The kiln was active between c.1170-1250 and it produced tableware, candlesticks, wine and water storage vessels and a variety of everyday items. [See T. B. Barry (1987), 57, 97].

Plate 2: Round headed windows: view of north window through south window.

the south east corner of the chancel in addition to a late medieval iron candlestick.[13]

Mausoleum

The mausoleum was built by the Butler family, probably in the late seventeenth or early eighteenth century. It is a rectangular building, now in ruin and roofless. The south wall is breached and it is here that access is gained to the interior [Plate 4]. The east gable is intact and

Plate 3: Romanesque church doorway in south wall.

Plate 4:   Mausoleum, south wall.

contains a long and narrow bricked-up window. The west gable is in a better state of preservation and the doorway within it, now bricked-up, is clearly visible. The north wall also has a bricked-up opening which appears to have been a large window. Large slab stones indicate the vault entrance. In the 1950s or 60s the west gable doorway was built up by Tipperary (S. R.) Co. Council and the vault was sealed. In 1982, the south wall was breached by the Co. Council, the undergrowth was removed and the vault entrance was excavated. No memorial slabs or inscriptions were found, only a handful of human bones.[14] Mrs. Aighleann O'Shaughnessy, then Assistant Inspector of National Monuments for the OPW inspected the vault and concluded that archaeological excavations were not worthwhile.[15] By 1991, the vault cover was damaged and the Co. Council was concerned about desecration.[16] At this time we took the opportunity of descending its narrow steps to the damp room below. The underground space measures about two and a half by two metres and is two metres high. The vault was subsequently resealed and there is now no access.

Though there is no remaining archaeological evidence to indicate who is interred in the mausoleum, historical sources indicate that among the Butler burials are Col. Thomas Butler of Kilcash (d. 1738), Margaret Butler, Lady Iveagh (d. 1744), Archbishop Christopher Butler (d. 1757), Walter Butler, 16th Earl of Ormonde (d. 1773) and John Butler, 17th Earl of Ormonde, (d. 1795). Local tradition records how in

1848 a leaden mitre (marking the burial-place of Archbishop Christopher) was removed from the mausoleum by nationalists wishing to make bullets.[17]

The mausoleum is described in the *Ordnance Survey Name Books* of 1840 as 'a burying place consisting of 4 walls roofed and slated like a house having no door or window except a very small aperture in each gable'.[18]

Graveyard

The information from a cataloguing of the legible grave inscriptions (dating from 1691 to 1986) is recorded in Appendices 1 and 2 while the approximate positions of the recorded graves are plotted in Illustration 4. Scattered around the graveyard are low rocks; these may be grave markers of the poor, boundary markers or stones fallen from the nearby walls. Where it is impossible to determine which of the aforementioned applies, the rocks have not been recorded in the appendices.

A clear notion of the changing fashions in headstones can readily be determined from even a quick perusal of the graveyard. The most interesting stones are those which are carved with emblems reminiscent of Penal crosses,[19] representatives of a tradition in Church art which had its origins in pictorial compositions of the mid-fifteenth century.[20] Such passion symbols depict various items associated with the crucifixion of Jesus: the cross, a ladder, a hammer and nails, the

Plate 5:   Detail from headstone of "Kilmurry School"
Details from L-R: Hammer & tongs, stars & moon, whip, cock who crows for Peter (standing on the scourging pillar), tongs, dice of soldiers, lance, cups to catch blood, vinegar sponge, cross, ladder, seamless robe, flail, thirty silver pieces (with bag above cross on right), tomb with rock door. [Grave number 68 in appendices]

Plate 6: Worn grave slab with chalked passion symbols. [Grave no. 31 in appendices].

thirty pieces of silver, the tomb and the spear that pierced his side.[21] These stones represent a developed trend which seems to have been focused in the Kilsheelan-Kilmurry area from around 1721 to 1764.[22] In the Kilcash graveyard such headstones fall into two groups representing distinctive treatments of the same material. There are four headstones similar to Plate 5 and two similar to Plate 6.[23]

The Castle

The standing remains of Kilcash Castle, a short distance eastwards of the graveyard, consist of a tower house with a portion of the ruined south wall of a house which was added at a later date (see below).[24] The tower – a six storey building (if one includes the room in the pitch of the roof) of sandstone and limestone – is currently in ruins, awaiting maintenance work by the State to preserve it from collapsing. It is one of about 400 tower houses which survive in Tipperary.[25] Archaeological evidence suggests that the tower was substantially remodelled at various stages during its long history and it is not always easy to identify or date certain of its features.[26] A general trend in the castle's history from defensive capability towards comfort and the associated dictates of fashion can, however, be observed.

It is probable that the tower originally had a bawn, a stone walled enclosure which played some part in the defence of the tower, but which was more important in protecting animals from thieves[27] and predators such as wolves.[28] Certainly there was one in the 1650s when the *Civil Survey* was taken.[29] Considered as a whole, the castle does not appear to have been *remodelled* with military calculations in mind, despite the martial history of its inhabitants. Though the tower still has some features associated with fortification, its sizeable windows preclude its serving a mainly defensive purpose.

Plate 7: Kilcash Castle from the north west

The Tower Exterior

Historical sources indicate that the tower house was built between 1538 and 1545.[30] The outer walls of the tower, in common with most similar structures,[31] are composed of rubble walls with well-cut quoins (dressed cornerstones). The walls remain intact, although the south wall is in a dangerous condition. Someone has cut the bottom of the once flourishing ivy so that it will do no further damage to the stonework. Despite the tower's remaining defensive features (see below) there are no surviving crenellations or merlons, though they were surely battlements on the tower when it was built.* These have either fallen away or they were thrown down to reduce the military capacity of the building.[32] One can still walk around the alure (the walkway around the rooftop) however this is precarious as the parapet (the wall running around the alure) is often missing and the walls are subsiding. Even the drip stones† around the top of the tower are for the most part decayed to the extent that they are hardly visible.

---

*Crenellations and merlons are parts of the battlements. Merlons are the solid upright sections while crenellations are he spaces between the merlons. In Irish battlements the crenellations were often 'stepped'.

†Drip stones protrude from outer walls to let rainwater drain away in such a fashion that the water does not merely stream down the wall.

PLAN OF KILCASH CASTLE 1997
SCALE: ———— =10M

COTTAGES

MODERN BOUNDARY

TOWER
INTERIOR 6 X 7.6M

LENGTH 13.4M
HEIGHT 18.2M

REMAINS OF HALL WALL

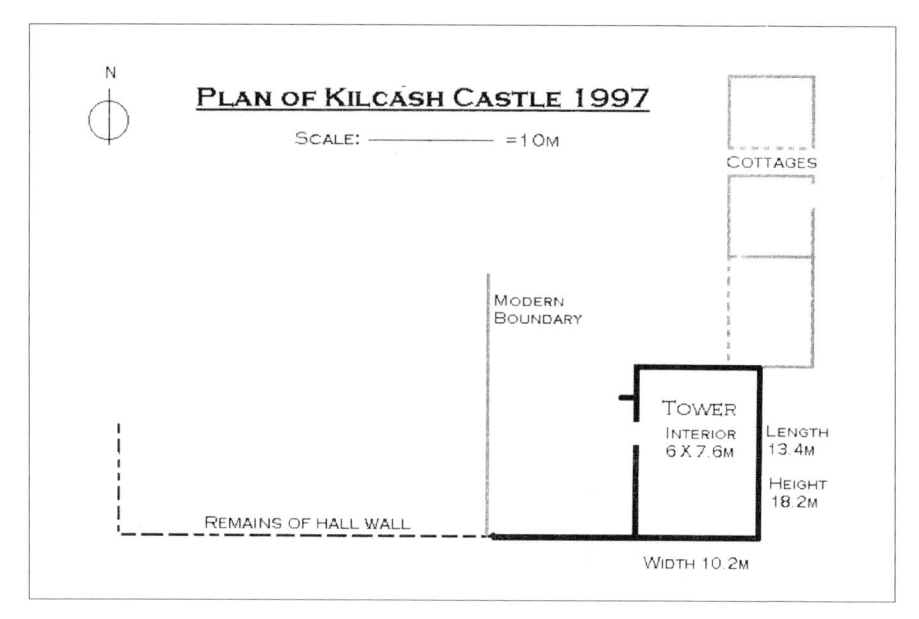

WIDTH 10.2M

Illus. 1:   Dimensions of the castle ruins.

In addition to rectangular loop windows (the majority of which have had their limestone finishing hacked away) there are three large windows on each of the north, south and east walls. These measure approximately 2.7m high by 1m wide and were probably late features of the tower representing a move towards human comfort at the expense of defensibility. When the tower was first built these may have been embrasures (recesses) occupied by much smaller windows which were subsequently enlarged to their present size, though sixteenth century tower-houses did occasionally have larger windows in their upper levels. Like the loops on the south wall these are sometimes blocked up. The only mullions (the solid uprights between the panes of glass in a window) remaining are in the window on the top of the east wall, which like its partner in the south wall, also has its hood-moulding (the narrow stone projection over the window) largely intact.

The base of the east wall has the remains of a later building which seems to have been built up against the tower for some indeterminate purpose. At ground level the tower also has two rectangular horizontal windows (measuring 53.5cm x 25cm) which once had iron grilles. These windows would have opened into embrasures in the inside of the tower. At some date after the construction of the tower however, the interior wall behind these windows was partially built up so that they are now filled in.[33] On the same wall, to the north of the large windows on each of the upper levels, there is an oculus, a small round window untypical of tower houses and another indication of the tower's relatively late construction.

At the top of the north wall are the remains of a chimney and on the north west corner is a machicolation* which is in good repair, its apertures which allowed the tower's inhabitants to fire at attackers ('musket loops') still clearly visible. [Plate 10] At ground level there is a small blocked up horizontal window similar to those on the east wall. The north wall also bears the remains of a section of decorative plaster which has a regular design (two parallel lines supporting a wavy line) running along its length. Near the north east end the walls of the tower show where the adjoining buildings were once keyed in to the tower wall. These later buildings, now almost wholly ruined where they meet the tower, seem once to have been accessible from the staircase in the tower interior (see below). However, the doorway has now been blocked up.

The west wall has the entrance doorway to the tower (2.1m high at centre by 1.14m wide) which has two small apertures in its frame (one on its left hand side and one at the apex of its arch) which were for the chains which secured the yett, a metal grille which protected the main point of entry to the house.[34] [Plate 8]. The dressed stone on the south side of the doorway has been damaged and replaced. This was possibly as a result of the rusting of the iron hinges of the yett (or of the hinges being pulled away) and damaging the stonework. The rough repair to the doorway would not have been evident after the house was added to the tower as the whole doorway was plastered over and to-day the remains of more than one layer of plaster are still visible in places.

Directly over the doorway, at the top of the tower, is a well preserved box machicolation [Plate 9]. This defensive feature proves that the tower was an earlier construction than the house, as the machicolation was obviously redundant after the house was constructed. There are the remnants of three chimneys on this west wall [Plate 9b], as well as the purlin holes (holes which once held rafters or other supports) for the beams of the roof of the attached building.

The south wall [Plates 11 & 16], which has the remains of a relieving arch at its base, is in particularly bad condition. One evening in August 1922 during the Civil War, General Prout (of the Free State army), advancing from the direction of Ballyneale, shelled the castle with an

---

*A machicolation projects from the walls of a building to allow defenders to shoot downwards on attackers. They can be found where two walls meet (a 'corner machicolation') or on a single wall.

18-pound gun, suspecting it to be occupied by Republican forces, and this, it appears, is responsible for some of the damage to the top of the wall as at least one shell hit the building.[35] The south-east of the tower has the remains of a second, rounded, corner machicolation which is substantially more damaged than its partner on the north east. It has been suggested to us that the lower part of this wall may date from before the construction of the rest of the tower, though this awaits the further analysis of an archaeological survey.[36]

Plate 8: Entrance doorway – note the holes to secure the yett to the left and top of the door

Though the four walls of the castle have batters,* the south east corner has an additional buttress with carved quoins. Examination of this buttress shows it to have been an addition to the south wall of the tower. Quoins appear to have been taken from elsewhere and incorporated into the buttress as the quoin at ground level on its west side has an otherwise incongruous chamfer (a 'flattened' or bevelled edge). The buttress seems to be unfinished insofar as there are keying in stones on its west side, an indication of an unfulfilled intention.[37]

On the exterior of the south west of the tower at about the level of the first floor there is clear indication that a section of the wall has been refilled and rendered over. It has been suggested that this aperture contained the chute for the garderobe (toilet). As garderobes went out of fashion and chamber pots were introduced the tower's inhabitants evidently felt it incumbent on them to remove the evidence of more primitive sanitary arrangements (which in any case appear to have discharged on to what became the front lawn).[38]

---

*A batter is the thickening of a wall towards its base. This buttressed the wall as well as causing missiles dropped from the tower to rebound outwards. [H. G. Leask (1951), 20].

Plate 9a: West wall – machicolation above door.

Plate 9b: West wall chimneys (viewed from the east).

The Tower Interior

On entering the doorway, there is a small room for the door-keeper immediately to the right. At the back of this guard-room there is a small niche while on the wall near the door there is a low musket loop (now blocked) which would have allowed the castle's inhabitants to fire out at any attackers. The archway leading into this room indicates that the wall has been remodelled at some point after its construction. Over the doorway is a murder hole, the aperture of which has been filled in with concrete [Plate 12].

Immediately inside the doorway, on the left hand side, a seam which shows where the wall was rebuilt can be clearly seen. It appears likely that in the original tower there was a passage here which joined with the passage on the north wall.[39] This L-shaped passage-way would have provided access to the stairs. The remodelling makes it impossible to determine how exactly the entrance lobby of the castle was designed. On entering there was certainly a door to the right and to the left (to give entry to the sentry-box and to the stairs passage respectively). An additional door immediately in front of the entrance probably gave access to the ground floor. Alternatively, the entrance may have been through the stairs passageway.

The ground level has a rocky earthen floor and a large fireplace in the south wall. This fireplace seems originally to have been an

Plate 10:   Corner machicolation – north east.

embrasure which was converted to its subsequent use with the addition of a small flue on its east side. In common with all of the fireplaces in the building, with the exception of that on the fifth floor (which was inaccessible) this fireplace has had its lintel removed. The presence of the fireplace shows that later in the castle's history the ground floor was not merely a store as was often the case in tower houses.[40]

Bearing in mind the now blocked up horizontal windows on the exterior of the east wall of the tower, it seems that there were two embrasures in the east wall which were subsequently filled in. What may have been the archway of the embrasure in the south east may still be seen, though it is also possible that this arch was a part of the later filling in of the wall. There are clearer indications of an embrasure in the west wall which may once have had a horizontal window – similar to those still on the east and north walls – which was blocked up during the construction of the house.

Today, though the often paired corbels are for the most part in place none of the wooden floors remain [Plate 15]. These corbels would have supported wooden beams called 'wall plates' which ran the length of the wall and which in turn supported the beams of the floor. In consequence, 'When looking at the floorless castle today, the observer must picture in his mind the missing floor levels at from twenty inches to two feet over the corbels which still jut out from the walls.'[41]

Plate 11: View of castle from south east.

The tower's floors were all made of wood. There is no stone vault in the tower, a vault being a feature particularly associated with earlier castles as it had both defensive and fireproofing purposes.[42] Wooden partitions may have further divided up the various floors, providing some privacy for the castle's inhabitants.[43]

The west wall, overhead the door, is over two metres thick. Above the ground floor the wall is hollow and in the first and subsequent floors they house small intramural chambers on either side of the central fireplaces. Such chambers were usually found in the wall which faced the bawn as they weakened the wall and thus were positioned where they were less open to attack.[44] In the absence of a ladder the chambers are no longer accessible, though one can see into them from the roof and from the doors which once gave onto the various floors. The chambers on the north side – each originally lit by a single loop window – are small, measuring less than two metres long by one metre wide. Those on the south side are L-shaped, passing round the south west corner where their loop was on the short leg of the L. It is likely that at the level of the first floor at least, the L-shaped intra-mural chamber in the south-west corner served as a garderobe.

Plate 12: Murder hole.

The spiral staircase in the north east corner winds up eighty-four even steps opening out through doorways which once gave access to the castle's living chambers. The stairs itself is in good repair, being solid and easily climbed. It is now accessed through a low entry hall in the north wall which is roofed with rough sharp stones which are visible, the lime and sand plaster having fallen away. If one looks carefully, some of the wattle, centuries old, can be seen on the roof of the passageway.

As one begins to climb the steps there is a rebuilt area of wall to the north which suggests that there was once a doorway between the tower and the adjoining buildings (now in ruins). The stairs is lit by loops, most of which have been stripped of their finishing; however some loops in better repair do remain and some of the loops have recesses below them which indicate that they were musket loops. The walls on either side are plastered for most, though not all, of its ascent. The plaster stops before the fifth floor which does not seem to have been used in the tower's latter years as its fireplace, all of its windows and its intramural chambers are bricked up.

The staircase gave access to the various floors through pointed arched doors, which – like the loops and windows – are now missing most of their original dressed stone. The arches of the doors often remain, while the uprights on either jamb are absent, probably because the arches were less amenable to incorporation into other buildings. In the remaining stones at the bases on the east side of the doorway there are holes for door pivots. Further marks around the doorways suggest that iron rather than stone hinges were used. On the eastern wall there is a noticeable rebate which would have allowed one to open back the door fully. The stairs terminates at the caphouse at roof level, rewarding the climber with an impressive view of the surrounding countryside.

Plate 13: Doorway off stairs.

The House

The house adjoining the tower is by no means unique to Kilcash. Richard Stanihurst, writing in the sixteenth century, describes the Gaelic Irish as having 'big and spacious palaces made of white clay and mud' adjacent to their towers. These buildings would have been thatched and thus the family of the castle would have slept in the more secure confines of the tower.[45] The Anglo-Irish sometimes built more sturdy constructions next to some of their towers and in some cases, such as at Athclare in Co. Louth, the adjoining construction was built at the same time as the tower.[46]

The remains of the south wall of 'an extensive dwelling house in

Plate 14:   Inside of north wall viewed from the south. Exit to roof on right.

ruins' (to use a description of 1840)[47] consists of three bays extending for 11.4m of its original length. This is confirmed by a copy of a drawing of the building which was done by James Fogarty in 1851 [Illustration 2].[48] The base of what remains of the rest of the wall has become incorporated into a boundary ditch. The house was a two storey building with a loft in the roof which could be accessed through a door which was knocked through the west wall of the tower house. The lower half of the wall of the hall was noticeably thicker than the upper story and it was thus that the floor was supported.

The two westernmost windows on the upper floor help date the house. The big flat-headed windows and their stonework date from the Tudor period.[49] A farther indication of the windows' date can be gleaned from the false stonework in the exterior plasterwork to the right hand side of the top westernmost window. This may originally have been painted black.[50] It can clearly be seen where these windows were narrowed in the eighteenth century to remodel them to more fashionable proportions. The top window on the east, nearest the tower has not been narrowed and may have been added to the house when the other windows were reduced in size. Alternatively, it may have been an original, though smaller window which was subsequently enlarged.

The large windows in the ground floor of the house are featureless

Plate 15: Interior of tower.
View from the ground floor facing north. The large windows of the north wall are clearly visible as are the various doorways opening out into what were once the tower's floors. At the top the remaining fireplace – saved by its inaccessibility – is in good condition. The top of the picture can be seen from a different angle in Plate 14.

Plate 16: South wall of house and tower.

and thus impossible to date with certainty. It is possible that they took their present form in the late seventeenth or the eighteenth century and the rotting timbers which now precariously support the remains of the floor above them seem to date from this phase.[51]

Along the top of the wall are a regular series of square holes, resembling putlog holes. These are likely to have held wooden brackets for a cornice to hold a projecting eave, a late seventeenth century[52] feature found at Kilmacurragh (Co. Wicklow) and Eyrecourt (Co. Galway).[53]

The north wall of the house has been almost completely removed. A small section of it juts out from the west side of the tower-house. At its lower level the stonework suggests that a door to the house was situated here, near to the door to the tower, though one might expect that the main door was in the centre of the north wall. The earlier dimensions of the house can be imagined from the remaining section of the north wall and from the declivity which runs along its original length out into what is now a field. It must have been a great building indeed with fireplaces (the remains of a flue can be seen on the west wall of the tower) and a large stairs. There were internal divisions (probably of wood) of which no trace remains though the historical record shows that there was a great hall.[54] Sadly, the rest of its detail can only be speculated on.

Plate 17: The oven, to the east of the tower.

Plate 18: Standing gable of outbuilding viewed from north east.

Plate 19: Standing gable of outbuilding viewed from south west.

Other Buildings

Little now remains of the other buildings near the castle. To the north of the tower, only a few metres away, there are the ruins of two low buildings. Looking at the north face of the tower and examining the ground between it and the first building suggests that there was once another structure joining it to the tower. These buildings have been rebuilt on several occasions and are difficult to date.

On the eastern boundary of the field to the east of the tower is the remaining gable of a bake house. A brick-lined oven which may date from the late seventeenth or eighteenth century can clearly be seen [Plate 17]. Today, the oven is higher than it would have originally been, as its flagged floor has been removed (the level of the original floor can be determined by the remains of a few flags protruding from the wall of the oven). Ovens such as these were often heated by burning furze in them. The ashes were then swept out and as the bricks retained their heat the oven could then be used for baking bread.[55]

Illus. 2: A drawing of Kilcash Castle in 1851.

Farther east of the oven are four large walled gardens. The west and south walls of the gardens are lined in a red brick which would have retained the heat of the sun necessary for growing certain plants. These gardens do not appear on the Ordnance Survey of 1840 though they most likely date from sometime in the eighteenth century, a period when ornamental gardens were planted all over Ireland.[56] We know, for example, that one of Thomas Butler's son-in-laws, George Mathew of Thomastown, was completing a mansion with formal gardens around 1718.[57] The Butlers of Kilcash may have been inspired by the example of the Kilkenny branch of the family. As early as the latter half of the

1600s Kilkenny castle had impressive formal gardens complete with French gardener and fountains.[58] It is also possible that the plateau visible in the field to the south of the tower house at Kilcash may represent the remains of some type of landscaping.

Beyond the west of what would once have been the gable of the house stands the remains of a building which is now of indeterminate function [Plates 18 & 19]. It may once have been contiguous with the house. It appears to have been a three story construction (including the pitch of the roof) the middle story of which had some fine windows on the gable (which are missing their lintels in common with the windows of the castle). Between these windows was the ivy-clad remains of a fireplace and chimney flue. Most of this gable collapsed during a storm in 1998 after we photographed it.

In James Fogarty's 1851 drawing of the castle this building is called a 'chapel' and it has a door in its south face and windows on the first floor [see Illustration 2]. What evidence Fogarty had for this is not known. However, it seems likely that either the devout Richard or Thomas Butler had a private chapel for Catholic worship.[59]

References

1. Monument number TI078-03601 in *Sites and Monuments Record: County Tipperary South Riding*, [Geraldine Stout et al. (1992)].
2. Michael O'Flanagan ed. (1930/1840), 55-6.
3. In 1999 three carved Romanesque stones with roll mouldings were still to be found in the rubble in the nave.
4. Conversation with Con Manning.
5. P. D. Sweetman (1984), 41.
6. For the latter see ibid., 36. The former date has been suggested to us by Con Manning because of the presence of antae.
7. Council MS. Letter from D. M. G. Holland, B. Eng. to Aighleann O'Shaughnessy, (Assistant Inspector of National Monuments, OPW), 18/8/1982, (in which Mr Holland opines that it 'might fall in the next storm') and Patrick Holland (1983), 4.
8. P. D. Sweetman (1984), 42.
9. Patrick Holland writes that it 'is definitely dated to post 1127-1134' [(1983), 4]. P. D. Sweetman dates the Romanesque doorway to the third quarter of the twelfth century [(1984), 42].
10. Patrick Holland (1983), 5.
11. Dúchas MS. Letter dated 30/5/84 from P. D. Sweetman to Mr Danaher, Chief Architect OPW [in files of Department of Arts, Heritage, Gaeltacht and the Islands].
12. Sweetman does not mention the candlestick in his article of 1984. However, in a letter dated 30/5/84 from P. D. Sweetman to Mr Danaher of the OPW [in Dúchas MS.] the candlestick is recorded.
13. Council MS. Letter to Patrick Holland, Museum Development Organiser, Clonmel from D. M. G. Holland, Environmental Section, Tipperary (S. R.) County Council dated 23/8/1985.
14. Council MS. Letter to Mrs K. M. Lanigan, Dublin Rd., Kilkenny from Clonmel

from D. M. G. Holland, Environmental Section, Tipperary (S. R.) County Council dated 23/8/1985.
15. Council MS. Internal memo to Peter O'Donoghue, A/EE, 18/11/91.
16. Thurles MS. *Irish Tourist Association Topographical & General Survey, Barony of Iffa and Offa east, Parish of Kilsheelan & Kilcash, Form A*, dated 3/10/1942. See also Patrick Power (1912), 149.
17. Michael O'Flanagan ed. (1930/1840), 204.
18. See Niall E. McKeith (1995), 27-30 and Francis Joseph Bigger (1909), passim.
19. Helen Roe (1983), 529.
20. A pictorial guide to these symbols can be found in Fergus O'Farrell (1983) and in Diarmuid O'Keeffe (1998), 200-3.
21. Thus Diarmuid O'Keeffe (1998), 200 correcting A. K. Longfield (1954). O'Keefe [ibid., 212] provides a list of such stones in the area along with their locations and approximate dates.
22. These are numbered in the appendices as follows. The group of four: numbers 17, 19, 20, and 68. The group of two: numbers 6 and 31. Diarmuid O'Keefe (1998), 212 only identifies one gravestone of the second type, having missed number 6.
23. Monument number TI078-037 in *Sites and Monuments Record, County Tipperary South Riding* [Geraldine Stout et al. (1992)].
24. Conrad Cairns (1987), 3.
25. Mike Salter (1993), 115.
26. See Conrad Cairns (1987), 21; Tom McNeill (1997), 217. 'Bawn' is the Irish equivalent of the 'bailey'. Mike Salter notes the presence of the bawn [(1993), 115].
27. Wolves remained a problem in Ireland well into the seventeenth century. The English poet Sidney (d. 1586) mentions the practice of several English nobles who sent for them for their parks. [Katherine Duncan-Jones (1991), 123]. During the food shortages of 1603, wolves were reported as attacking the enfeebled populace [E. Margaret Crawford ed. (1989), 10.] In 1614 the King granted a bounty for the destruction of Irish wolves [Conrad Cairns (1994), I, 53].
28. Con Manning has suggested to us that part of the bawn may survive to either side of the current entranceway.
29. Robert C. Simington ed. (1931), 271.
30. Patrick C. Power (1976), 44, n. 24 q.v. Conrad Cairns suggests a date of c. 1540 [Conrad Cairns (1994), I, 395].
31. Conrad Cairns (1994), I, 202.
32. The 'slighting' of a castle in the Cromwellian era often involved the throwing down of the parapet and the breaching of the wall. [H. G. Leask (1951), 19]. Michael Gavin Senior of Ballypatrick (b. 11/4/13) recalls that in the early years of the century, local children playing in the castle used throw stones down from the roof.
33. These might have served as openings for small breech-loaded cannon. However, the presence of a grille would seem to militate against this. Certainly, such square openings for cannons were not unknown in Ireland in castles of the 1540s [Paul M. Kerrigan (1995), 26-27. See especially Fig. 27. Also ibid., 19 for a diagram of the cannon] and we know that the Butlers were in possession of such weapons [Ibid., 24.].
34. The bore of the hole at the apex of the arch and its position make it unlikely that it is a musket loop. A similar arrangement can be seen in Tom McNeill (1997), 219, fig. 131.

35. Conversation with Michael Gavin senior (b. 11/4/13) of Ballypatrick, Clonmel, who lived nearby the castle at the time. Mr Gavin remembers that at least three shells were fired at the castle, one of which made its mark while the others landed in neighbouring fields. The local children found the remains of the shells where they landed. See also Carlton Younger (1970), 400.

    During the Civil War the area around the castle was a regular haunt of the IRA. Up to a dozen IRA members might be in the castle at any one time. Neighbouring children used visit the soldiers and clean their guns in return for sweet cake or buns (which were in short supply). The Republicans sometimes had a road block on the main road south of the castle. Here, they would waylay delivery vans and redistribute the spoils to the families of the houses in which they billeted themselves. (On one occasion Mr Gavin remembers Dan Breen (1894-1969), one of the most wanted men in Tipperary, arriving at about ten o'clock at night and turning his grandmother out of her bed).
36. Conversation with Con Manning.
37. Conversation with Jean Farrelly.
38. Conversation with Jean Farrelly.
39. Conversation with Con Manning.
40. Tom McNeill (1997), 222.
41. H. G. Leask (1951), 82.
42. See Conrad Cairns (1987), 13-4; H. G. Leask (1951), 86.
43. Conrad Cairns (1987), 15.
44. Conrad Cairns (1987), 99.
45. Tom McNeill (1997), 221.
46. Ibid.
47. John O'Donovan (1930/1840), 56. In all cases O'Donovan's letters have been compared with the MS. copies in the RIA (*Ordnance Survey of Ireland, Antiquities, County of Tipperary, Letters* vol. 1). However, we cite page references to their reproductions as they are more accessible.
48. This faded MS. copy, executed by the daughters of Maurice Lenihan of Limerick, is in UCDF. The original does not seem to have survived. We are grateful to Con Manning for alerting us to the existence of this drawing.
49. Conversation with Con Manning. Conrad Cairns [(1987), 17] also dates the hall to the late sixteenth or early seventeenth century.
50. Conversation with Jean Farrelly.
51. Conversation with Con Manning.
52. As Con Manning has pointed out to us, this feature may suggest that the reshaping of the windows is late seventeenth century rather than eighteenth century. Of course, he continues, there may have been both a late seventeenth and an eighteenth century phase. [Letter to the authors 21/4/99].
53. Letter from Con Manning to the authors, 2/4/99. He refers to Maurice Craig's *Classic Irish Houses of the Middle Size* (1977, pp. 64-6) and The Knight of Glin et al. *Vanishing Country Houses of Ireland* (1988, p. 71).
54. Katherine M. Lanigan (1985), 397.
55. Conversation with Con Manning.
56. The *Ordnance Survey Letters* [John O'Donovan (1930/1840), 56] mention the remnants of impressive gardens.
57. Anne Crookshank (1986), 484.
58. Edward Malins & The Knight of Glin (1976), 6-7.
59. See the quotation from the preface of Paul of St Ubald in Chapter II.

Chapter II

The Early History of Kilcash

Old Kilcash: The Beginnings
The origins of the settlement at Old Kilcash are lost in a history which may reach back at least to *c.* 550 AD. Rev. W. P. Burke, writing at the end of the 1800s, speaks of the veneration of a tribal saint, Colman Mac Erc, who presided over a monastic foundation at Kilcash about the middle of the sixth century.[1] The *Annals of the Four Masters*, or *The Annals of the Kingdom of Ireland* (*Annála ríoghachta Éireann*, compiled between 1632-36) record the death in 846 AD of 'Diarmuid of Cill Caisi'[2] who Burke believes to have been an abbot who was a successor of Colman's.

Though Burke's hypothesis may in part be correct, from the laconic entry in the *Annals* it is impossible to be sure that *Cill Caisi* referred to is the Kilcash in Tipperary that we know today.[3] How conceivable it is that such confusion may come about is best illustrated by an entry in the *Red Book of Ormond* which lists the lands held by one Robert Purcell in February of 1308. Here, we read of 'a field of 66 acres stretching to Kilcaxe from the Suir'.[4] Such a small plot of land could hardly have stretched from the river to the hinterland of Kilcash, and as the rest of Robert Purcell's land is near Holy Cross (and thus near the Suir), it is more likely that it is some 'Kilcaxe' in this area which is being spoken of.[5] Amidst the profusion of Kylcasses, Kylcaxes, Kyllcaishes, Killkashes and other variations, it is not *always* possible to identify the Kilcash which concerns us.[6] Early modern sources list at least one 'Kilcash' in Roscommon and there is a 'Cill-Caisi' which is now Kilkeasy, near Knocktopher in Co. Kilkenny.[7]

It had long been though that *Cill Chais* was the Irish for 'Caise's Church'.[8] The identification of such a Caise and how (if at all) he relates to Colman, we will hardly ever know. The *Martyrology of Donegal* or *Calendar of Irish Saints* (*Félire na naomh nÉrennach*, 1630) which was prepared by Michael O'Clery (who begun the *Annals of the Four Masters*) has an entry for 'Cas, of Bennchar' on April the 26th.[9] Apparently, there was also an 'Old or forgotten saint of Ossory' called Cais or Caissi[10] and the *Genealogies of the Saints of Ireland* (*Corpus*

Genealogiarum Sanctorum Hiberniae) also lists a Saint Cass.[11] Which – if any – of these was the Cais of Kilcash, it is impossible to say.

To compound this difficulty, it seems likely that the place-name may not refer to a Caise at all. In fact the Irish might easily be translated as 'church near a rivulet' while recent research suggests that it is best translated as 'church of twistedness'.[12] This emphasises the difficulty of recovering any historical trace of the area in the early Christian period.

In addition, the physical records of any primitive settlements have long since been erased. Building with mortar was an innovation of the late eight and ninth centuries AD[13] and in a well wooded country like Ireland the earliest churches and houses would have been thatched and made of timber, a feature recorded by the Venerable Bede (673-735 AD).[14] If Burke is correct in surmising that Kilcash was a monastic foundation of the mid 500s it is worth noting that our modern view of such a foundation may be somewhat at variance with the historical reality as 'The monasteries were essentially secular and, for the most part, monks were laymen.'[15] Since many abbots were not members of the clergy they were often drawn from the families of the local ruling élite.

It is with a certain relief then that we turn to the stones of the old church for more solid historical foundations. A fairly recent excavation (1984) of the site under the auspices of the then Office of Public Works tells us that the chancel (the smaller, eastern part of the ruin) 'is hardly earlier than the twelfth century',[16] though perhaps this survey was mistaken and it is in fact as early as the tenth century.[17] We are not solely dependent on the dating of archaeology at this point however as around 1190-1200 AD we have a record of Baldwin Niger or Baldwin [the] Black giving the church and about 600 acres[18] to the hospital of the priory of St John the Baptist without the Newgate in Dublin.[19] There was some delay in the Hospital's taking over the church, as the Hospital records show a Rev. Walter de Valle ceding possession of it a century later in 1307-08.[20] These brief entries in the *Register of the Hospital of S. John the Baptist* provide us with the earliest certain references to Kilcash. The presence of Walter de Valle (doubtless a scion of the Wall family who were at the time the owners of Kilcash and of whom more will be said later) and the confirmation of the church transfer by John Leynagh, Bishop of Lismore (1325-54) establish the church's location with certainty. However, the *Register* fails to tell us who Baldwin Niger was and thus the early history of the manor of Kilcash has to be reconstructed speculatively.

The first Norman mercenaries landed in Ireland in late 1167 at the invitation of Diarmait Mac Murchada, the exiled king of Leinster. With the arrival of prominent nobles such as Richard fitz Gilbert, better known as Strongbow (d. 1176), the English Crown, in the person of Henry II (1133-89) was forced to focus attention on affairs in this country. Prince John, Lord of Ireland and the youngest son of Henry, was accompanied on his first expedition here by Theobald Walter (d. 1205), honorary butler to his household. The extensive grants of land (totalling 750,000 acres) which Theobald received in north Munster and in Leinster were the foundation of the fortunes of the Butler's of Ormond who were to dominate the history of the area for centuries to come.[21]

The settlement of such a vast area changed the social structure of Gaelic Ireland indelibly. Tipperary was divided into cantreds, territorial units often reflecting political divisions established before the English invasion.[22] These cantreds, which formed the basic secular and ecclesiastical administrative unit, provided the framework for the manorial system of land tenure by which land was held, exploited and defended. The manorial system involved the Butlers carving out fiefs of about 3,000 to 5,000 acres which were held by tenant knights who owed them military service. These fiefs were further subdivided into holdings farmed by free tenants and serfs.[23]

The English settlement marks the transition of the Irish church from one which was based on the monastic system to one based on parishes.[24] This transition would not always have been a smooth one and with Kilcash on the borderline of two dioceses the parish became the subject of a disagreement between the bishops of Cashel and Lismore. In January of 1260 the Pope decided that the spiritual rights of a number of chapels including Kilcash – as well as those in Kilsheelan and Clonmel – were to fall under the auspices of Lismore.[25]

It is tempting to believe that it is around the time of the shift from the monastic to the parish system and the foundation of the manor of Kilcash (presumably under Baldwin Niger) in the twelfth century, that the church was built to serve both as a status symbol and as an exercise of faith. The presence of the church is a good indication that there was a manor house nearby, as the two almost invariably accompanied one another, with the owner of the manor house controlling the possession of the church.[26] This manor house may have stood on or near the site of the present castle and it may have been made of wood. No trace of it remains today and so we conclude that it must have been destroyed or pulled down to make way for the present structure. If the original dwelling was even partially made of stone, its materials may have been incorporated in later buildings.

The presence of a manor house and a church does not allow us to infer that there was a village or any similar 'manorial centre' in the area. Though it has been argued that as the manor house would have been the governmental and economic heart of the area it would naturally have attracted such a settlement, it has also been pointed out that the existence of larger free tenants living on their own farms would have made nucleation less likely.[27]

At the end of the twelfth century then, Baldwin Niger was installed as tenant of the manor of Kilcash. Baldwin had enough resources at his disposal to make his pious grant of the local church and the accompanying land to the Hospital in Dublin 'for the love of God and holy Mary and Saint John the Baptist and for the salvation of my soul and those of my parents and brothers and sisters and children and lords and all my antecedents'.[28] Baldwin's prayers do not seem to have served the temporal interests of his family though, as all trace of him and his disappear from the records. By the early 1300s it is the family of Richard de Valle which is installed at Kilcash.[29]

Neither Baldwin Niger nor Richard de Valle were tenants-in-chief. In the thirteenth and fourteenth century Kilcash stood in the cantred of Iffowyn (later known as Iffa which became part of the barony of Iffa and Offa in the sixteenth century) in the diocese of Lismore. Iffowyn's local ecclesiastical government was at Kilsheelan and its manor was likewise at Kilsheelan or Clonmel.[30] Kilcash may have been a manor under the manor at Kilsheelan, just as Carrick mcGriffin (now Carrick-on-Suir) was in the early 1300s.[31] In Baldwin Niger's time the eastern half of Iffowyn was not under the control of the Butlers but under William de Burgo who had been granted the territory by Prince John sometime before 1189. De Burgo later extended his control to the western half of the cantred by means which are now obscure. Originally this had been granted by Prince John to John de St Michael and in 1192-3 it was regranted to a William Dencurt. How Dencurt lost the land to de Burgo we do not know,[32] but in 1279 Walter de Burgo exchanged the manor of Kilsheelan for land in Ulster and in 1281 King Edward granted the manor of Kilsheelan with the town of Clonmel to one Otto de Grandison.[33]

Given all of these shifts in power it is hardly surprising that Baldwin Niger's land passed into the ownership of the De Valles. Even had there been less fluctuation in local political affairs, the times were precarious at best. It is not our purpose to sketch the dangers of life in late medieval Ireland; it suffices to say that many of the earliest references which might refer to the locality are ones associated with crime (the proceedings of the legal system being one of the earliest features of Irish life to be documented under the Anglo-Normans). Thus, in 1359 Neyld and Richard O'Neill of 'Kylcasse' had their chattels seized and were hanged for some unnamed felony.[34] Maurice Carragh Tobin and William Monghan are before the courts in 1402-3 for having robbed four cows belonging to William Laynagh Wall of Kilcash.[35] In all likelihood William Wall in his day would not have been alone in suffering the loss of his animals; cattle-raiding was widespread and apart from its economic motivation – in that it enriched the thieves while impoverishing their enemies – it seems to have been a proof of manhood.[36] By the sixteenth century things were little better: Thomas O'Flaghey of Kilcash steals a horse at Ballydine, a crime which paled in comparison with the audacity of James Brennagh (alias Ní Kahirragh) of Kilcash who succeeded in stealing 120 cows and in killing one Oweyne O'Downyll.[37]

The de Valles of Kilcash and Dame Alice Kyteler

In the early 1300s it is the family of Wall or de Valle who rule over Kilcash. Richard de Valle is master of the place and, as we have seen, Walter de Valle is the priest of the local church until its transfer to the Hospital. Around this time, the church was valued at five pounds for the purpose of tithes.[38] Richard appears to have been a prominent knight as he served both as sheriff of Co. Waterford (where he must have held lands) in 1301-2 and as sheriff of Co. Tipperary in 1307-8.[39] Richard de Valle was dead by 1316 and one of his sons (of which he had at least three by his first wife Christiana), also called Sir Richard, took over Kilcash. This Sir Richard is recorded as holding the post of Sheriff of County Tipperary in 1321.

For all the contemporary status of the de Valle family, their fame is easily eclipsed by that of the elder Sir Richard's second wife, Dame Alice Kyteler (b. c. 1262–post 1324). Because of her groundbreaking trial (1324) which associated heresy and witchcraft[40] she has a position in European history making her, internationally, the best-known lady of Kilcash.[41] It is this Alice who is remembered in W. B. Yeats's 'Nineteen Hundred and Nineteen':

> There lurches past, his great eyes without thought
> Under the shadow of stupid straw-pale locks,
> That insolent fiend Robert Artisson
> To whom the love-lorn Lady Kyteler brought
> Bronzed peacock feathers, red combs of her cocks.[42]

What can be reconstructed of the life and personality of Dame Alice Kyteler may call to mind Dame Alyson, the celebrated Wife of Bath from the *Canterbury Tales* of Geoffrey Chaucer (c. 1343-1400). Alyson announces proudly that 'Housbondes at chirche dore I have had fyve….And all were worthy men in hir degree'.[43] Alice Kyteler's boast was only slightly less modest: she had at least four husbands, all of whom indeed were 'worthy men'. The first of them, a Kilkenny banker and money lender whom she must have married c. 1280, enjoyed the striking surname of Outlawe.[44] Later she married in turn, Adam le Blund of Callan, Richard de Valle of Kilcash and finally Sir John le Poer.

Alice's many marriages were not in themselves things to be wondered at. In her day, a woman born of a good family and possessed of an ever increasing fortune needed the protection of a husband. In consequence, wealthy widows commonly remarried, several times when necessary. Alice probably came of affluent Kilkenny merchant stock. The Kytelers were influential Flemish merchants first recorded in Kilkenny (probably in 'Flemingstown') in 1277.[45] It is most likely that her upbringing involved some training in the monetary and political skills which Alice was to deploy to such good effect later in her life. Early on it becomes apparent that she was a forceful woman. She seems to have been in a business partnership with her husband Adam le Blund (King Edward I owed the couple £500 which he had borrowed to finance the Scottish Wars)[46] and in 1316-17 she sued her stepson, the junior Richard de Valle, for her widow's portion, the life interest in one third of a number of properties, including that at Kilcash.[47]

It is probably because of actions like this lawsuit that Alice attracted accusations of witchcraft. One of the features of her case which may surprise us initially is that she was denounced by her own step-children for murdering some of their fathers and evilly enchanting others,[48] as she had apparently done to her fourth husband, le Poer, whose 'whole body was emaciated and whose nails and body hair had been caused to fall out'.[49] It is clear that Alice favoured William Outlawe, a son by her first husband who, like his father, was a money lender. His half-siblings and/or siblings felt that his mother was ransacking their patrimonies for the sake of her favourite and they clearly resented this.[50]

The complaints of Alice's children found a ready ear in the person of the newly arrived Bishop of Ossory, Richard de Ledrede, an English-born Franciscan who came to Ireland from Avignon where he had been consecrated by Pope John XXII in 1317.[51] Avignon had, in 1312, just witnessed the abolition of the once powerful Knights Templars* and thus heresy and sorcery were in the air while de Ledrede was

---

*The crusading order had been under investigation for some years before their abolition. Ostensibly, they were being tried for devil worship, though it is more likely that – like Alice – they attracted enemies due to their considerable wealth. The Grand Master of the Templars and his staff were executed in 1314.

there.[52] In addition, Pope John was an active believer in the malevolent power of sorcery and it was not unknown for him to charge bishops with such offences.[53] De Ledrede appears to have been genuinely zealous in his search for heterodoxy[54] and in his protection of ecclesiastical privilege. His personal piety, expressed not only in his heresy persecutions but in his devotional poetry (mainly addressed to the Virgin) may not be to the taste of some modern readers, but it does at least appear to have been sincere.[55]

When this enthusiastic cleric arrived in Ossory and announced an inquiry into the spiritual state of his diocese, Alice's enemies were not slow to come forward with their accusations. It reads as a catalogue of what became fairly typical popular belief about witchcraft. Alice was at the head of a band of heretical sorcerers who sacrificed dismembered animals to demons, distributing the body parts at cross-roads. She was involved in attempts to see into the future with demonic aid and she and her accomplices brewed potions in the skull of a decapitated thief; nefarious mixtures composed of ingredients such as hairs of people's buttocks and the clothes from dead, unbaptised infant boys.[56] Importantly, Alice also had dealings with a demon, an incubus[57] known as 'the Son of Art' or 'Robin the Son of Art' who appeared variously in the form of a cat, a hairy black dog or a Negro (*aethiopis*). In exchange for sexual intercourse and other services this demon heaped her with wealth.[58]

Essentially then, the accusations – in the form of these and other unlikely tales – returned to the question of Alice's financial affairs. It did not seem to concern anyone that it was somewhat contradictory to suggest that her money was derived from defrauding heirs of their legitimate rights while at the same time insisting that it was the ill-got gain of demonic intercourse. After all, if her incubus provided her with great riches, she hardly had to take the trouble to murder her husbands! As one prominent modern commentator has observed, 'All the charges, in fact, are designed to serve one and the same purpose: to show that Lady Alice had no right to her wealth'.[59]

Bishop de Ledrede was genuinely horrified that such a notorious malefactor should be at large in his diocese, and he duly reported the case to the Lord Chancellor of Ireland, brother Roger Outlawe, Prior of the Hospital at Kilmainham and head of the crusading order of the Hospitallers in Ireland. However, despite (or perhaps because of) the fact that the Chancellor owed de Ledrede a large sum of money, no action was forthcoming.[60] It seems that the Chancellor was a relative of Alice's son, William Outlawe,[61] but whatever the reason, the important fact remained that the Chancellor initially refused to intervene in the case.

Dame Alice was not going to prove an easy target. Such obstructions tend to whet the appetites of the zealous pursuer rather than diminish them though, since the wiles and resources of the Devil were known to be many. The Bishop therefore decided that he would intervene directly and he cited Alice to appear before himself on charges of heresy. She sensibly considered that it was more prudent to flee and so de Ledrede was forced to cite her favourite son William instead.

The Kyteler/Outlawe resources were far from being exhausted. The powerful seneschal of Kilkenny, Sir Arnold le Poer interceded on his friend William's behalf (again, it appears possible that he was related to Alice through her fourth husband, Sir John le Poer). When the seneschal's appeal was ignored he defied ecclesiastical authority and imprisoned the bishop,[62] causing uproar in Kilkenny as the city was placed under interdict, thereby denying the sacraments to its inhabitants for as long as the bishop was denied his liberty. The seventeen days that cleric spent in prison were not readily forgotten and years later de Ledrede had the seneschal excommunicated and imprisoned in Dublin where the unfortunate man died without the benefit of last rites.[63]

Evidently de Ledrede was a man filled with the obstinacy of the righteous. He returned with his complaint to Dublin where, finally, the courts of the King and the Archbishop found against Alice who had to flee to England to escape punishment. In doing so she avoided the fate of her associate Petronilla of Meath who was flogged and then burnt at the stake, the first person in Ireland to be thus executed for heresy.[64] In England (or perhaps farther afield) Alice ended her days in obscurity, the tenacious, but finally defeated victim of a system which was suspicious of any exercise of power by women.[65] Her son William was also unfortunate in that he had to spend a period in prison before undergoing a rigorous penance, which, amongst other things, involved his paying for the provision of a leaden roof for de Ledrede's cathedral, St Canice's[66] (a building the bishop lavished resources on. Ledrede's full-length effigy can be seen there today on the slab of his tomb, to the left of the altar).

As the fate of the unfortunate Sir Arnold le Poer demonstrates, the ramifications of the Kyteler affair rumbled on for quite some time after Alice fled. Our primary interest is in the turbulent life of this determined woman who was once the Lady of Kilcash, so we will not follow in detail the full unwinding of the story. Suffice to say that de Ledrede's admixture of enthusiasm and stubbornness – combined with the enemies he made during the playing out of the Kyteler affair – involved him, in his turn, being accused of wrongdoing and rebellion against the King, with the result that he spent many years in exile from

Ossory (at one stage even returning to Avignon to enlist the aid of the Pope) before he was able to return to his diocese where he died in 1360.[67]

Alice's stepson, Richard de Valle (the son of the senior Richard de Valle and his first wife Christina), had three sons that we know of, Walter, Gilbert and Philip.[68] It was Walter who succeeded both to the Kilcash estates and to the position of Sheriff of County Tipperary. He was no stranger to warfare, having served with his men in 1332-3 under Sir Anthony de Lucy, Chief Justiciar of Ireland (the representative of the king) against rebels in Munster. In October 1337 he came to a violent end. His family and the local family of Poers had been at odds for some time and had finally sworn a truce under oath. However, one day while Walter was returning from Clonmel (where he had been discharging his duty as Sheriff), a band of Poers fell upon him and his retinue and he was slain along with thirteen other members of his household. The times, as we have already noted, were certainly less than peaceful. Even before the advent of the Black Death in the mid fourteenth century, famine was increasingly prevalent in the country (from c. 1270) and the Bruce invasion of 1315-18 seriously disrupted national political affairs.[69] Walter's son Richard was still an infant and so family control passed to his mother, Anastasia le Bret who managed the estates on behalf of her grandchild and who was still in control of the de Valle fortunes as late as 1354.[70]

The succession at Kilcash can be traced through a pedigree of William Vale of Tullaghmaine (east of Callan in Co. Kilkenny) which is dated 1584.[71] After Walter's son Richard (last recorded in 1387), we read of Edmund de Valle who handed over to another Richard (the name was popular in the family) who was succeeded by Richard Oge, then by Edmund and finally by the William whose pedigree was being established. William Vale of Tullaghmaine's father, Edmund, must be the Edmund recorded as tenant of Kilcash in 1517[72] and it is in his time, or shortly afterwards, that Kilcash passed into Butler hands between 1540 and 1542.

The history of the Wall family in Kilcash does not end here. Apart from the de Valles of the manor there is evidence of other branches of the family in the area. In the early 1400s we read of William 'the Leinsterman' Vale living at Kilcash. He was succeeded by his young son, Thomas.[73] One Patrick Vale was in trouble with the law in 1521 for allegedly burning a house, two stacks of corn and other stores to the value of forty pounds.[74] After the hand-over to the Butlers the Tudor *Fiants* record pardons to Ellena Wale (a daughter of Edmund, the last Wall owner of Kilcash) in 1567 and to Thomas Walle m'Rickard of Kilcash in 1577.[75]

The Church in Kilcash before the Protestant Reformation
After Walter de Valle quit the rectorship of Kilcash in 1307-8 it remained in the hands of the Fratres Cruciferi order[76] (at their priory of St John the Baptist in Dublin) until the Reformation. The Hospital (also known as 'Palmers Hospital') had been founded before 1188, and was probably the largest in Ireland.[77] It would have looked at Kilcash in terms of the revenue it could yield and it would eventually have installed a priest in the parish to look after the spiritual needs of the locals.[78] Its Kilcash land was only one holding of many in Tipperary – including lands at Fethard, Kiltinan and Caher – where it eventually appropriated substantial holdings.[79] Because of the fluctuating value of agricultural produce the Hospital was later to lease its land, thereby ensuring a more stable income. In 1443 for example, Brother Richard Walsh leased all of the Hospital land in Tipperary at the rate of ten marks a year, an arrangement which was contracted to stand for the duration of his life.[80]

During this time there is little or no record of the church at Kilcash though there was evidently some minor ecclesiastical problem there at the end of the fourteenth century as the parish was fined 12d.[81] For some time before the Reformation the monasteries of Ireland had been in decline, a fact which was reflected in the hospital of St John the Baptist in its bed numbers which decreased from 155 in the early 14th century to 50 on the eve of its dissolution in February 1539. When suppression came its most immediate affect was felt in the Pale and in Ormond lands (as monasteries survived in Gaelic areas for some time). Monks, like Sir Thomas Everarde, the last prior at St John the Baptist, were pensioned off and the possessions of the monastery (1,700 acres in various counties, including the Hospital's remaining land at Kilcash), reverted to the Crown.[82]

The Butlers and Kilcash: Early Connections
The mid-sixteenth century witnessed two important changes in the life of the manor of Kilcash. Firstly, either the last of the de Valles or the first of the Butler inhabitants of the manor erected the tower-house, the history and structure of which we have examined in Chapter I. Secondly of course, the manor passed from the hands of the de Valles into the possession of the Butlers.

Before this time there had already been some traffic between Kilcash and the Earls of Ormond. In 1387, Richard de Valle of Kilcash transferred land in Bellaghdirr (Co. Tipperary), to James the 3rd Earl.[83] Previously, in 1381, one Thomas de Valle, a member of the collateral branch of the family, had granted land in Kilcash to the head of the Ormond family.[84] The best known incident which connects the

Ormonds with Kilcash in the early period though, is probably the drawing up of the *Statutes of Kilcash* of 1474 or 1478.[85]

The *Statutes of Kilcash* are so called because they were agreed 'apud Ballikylcasse', that is at Kilcash, and not because they concerned the government of the surrounding region. Promulgated by James Butler, then deputy to the Earl of Ormond, the *Statues* were a quasi-legal ordinance which existed outside the common law and which seem to have been influenced by Brehon law. They were not the first instances of such legislation as James, the 'White Earl' (between 1411-1452) had, earlier in the century, enacted ordinances in various places and at various times mainly to regulate the system of coign and livery (the practice of billeting soldiers and other employees on tenants).[86]

The Kilcash *Statues* are somewhat different though. Firstly, they were not related to the question of coign and livery.[87] Secondly, unlike the earlier ordinances they were not enacted to consolidate a position of strength and stability in Tipperary as the Irish glory days of the White Earl were over by 1478. This was in part due to the execution of the White Earl's successor, James (the 5th Earl), who backed the wrong side (the Lancastrians) at the battle of Towton in Yorkshire (1461) during the English War of the Roses. Thus the man who had been Lord Deputy of Ireland and Lord High Treasurer of England ended his days with his head displayed on London bridge. The sixth and seventh Earls, John and his younger brother Thomas (d. 1515), were absent from Ireland and as a result, internal family feuds cast the Butler lordship into chaos.[88]

It is in this context that the *Statues* are to be understood. Their full intention is not clear as the manuscript copy of them which survives in the National Library of Ireland (written by Richard Howat, a clerk of Lisronagh) is in parts illegible.[89] Their general purpose seems to be the provision of safe passage along roadways and the prevention of ambushes. They were regulations for troubled times and it is possible that Kilcash was chosen for enacting them as it represented a neutral or convenient venue for the meeting of the concerned parties (which included the Butlers of Dunboyne and Cahir as well as the Archbishop of Cashel and the Bishop of Lismore).[90] As late as 1537 and the reign of Henry VIII the statutes were still being appealed to in local disputes.[91]

The Butlers of Kilcash

By the mid-sixteenth century then, the Butlers are no strangers to Kilcash. The dating of the hand-over from the de Valles to Ormond can be ascertained with some accuracy as a list of Ormond lands of 1538 does not mention Kilcash while the manor is mentioned in a will dated 1545, of James, the 9th Earl.[92] The acquisition of Kilcash is in keeping with the general shift of Butler power – beginning in the fourteenth century – from their original base around Nenagh in North Tipperary, to a reconsolidated position in South Tipperary and Kilkenny.[93] James seems to have appointed a relative as administrator for his newly acquired manor, as in 1542 Richard Fitz William Butler of Kylcaise is a signatory of a complaint made by some local notables to Henry VIII.[94] Two years later, this 'Richard Fitzwilliam' is recorded as Constable of Kilcash.[95]

With the death of the 9th Earl in 1546, Kilcash passed to his third son, Sir John, whose brother 'Black Tom' (who built the Tudor manor at Carrick-on-Suir) became the 10th Earl. John, like so many members of his family, appears to have led an event-filled life. As we would expect given of the position of the Butlers, he was a prominent figure in Munster in the 1550s and early 1560s. In 1559 we read of his receiving a royal pardon for some misdemeanour or another which was most likely something to do with the family feud against the neighbouring Geraldines.[96] Between April and July 1562 the Earls of Ormond (Black Tom) and Desmond were at the English court in an attempt to settle their differences. Nonetheless, hostilities between the two soon broke out again and in December 1563 Ormond complained to Sussex (Governor of Ireland) that 'John of Desmond and his men never cease burning, preying, and killing [my] tenants'.[97] At the time Sussex noted: 'Ormond's brother John…wounded and not likely to live'.[98] The extent of the troubles are best appreciated in the light of the findings of a Royal Commission which was eventually set up to arbitrate between Ormond and Desmond. The Commission found that Desmond should compensate his foe for the loss of 9,875 cattle, 804 stud mares, 2,827 plough 'gerranes',* 4,458 swine, 9,841 sheep and goats in addition to 2,747 pounds of damage to goods and the lives of 140 people who had been slain.[99] Eventually, in 1565, Desmond was defeated and taken prisoner by Ormond at the Battle of Affane (Co. Waterford) after which both of the Earls were summoned, once again, to mediation in London.

John was married to Katherine McCarthy Reagh and they had two sons – James (who died young) and Walter – and three daughters; Joan, Eleanor and Katherine. It is possible that John also had had another daughter, Margaret[100] and an illegitimate son, Thomas (who would not have been born before his father died).[101] There is difficulty in dating John's death precisely as Carte records that Walter was only six months old when his father (who is buried in St Canice's in

---

*From the Irish *gearrán*, 'a small and inferior kind of horse' [OED].

Kilkenny) passed away in May 1570.[102] On the other hand, there is evidence that John perished within a year of the wounds he received in 1563.[103]

Walter Butler of Kilcash (1559?-1632/3)

As he was a young child when his father died, Walter was brought up under the guardianship of his uncle, Black Tom, the 10th Earl (1531-1614). During Walter's minority the Earl controlled his nephew's patrimony of Kilcash. We are reminded that the estate had more than one church associated with it as in 1570 Black Tom granted the church of Kilconill in Cashel to Rev. Sir William Phelan.[104] Though the Earl was a Protestant, Walter remained a Catholic and it has been suggested that he was fostered in the Gaelic manner.[105] He was soon identified with the military manoeuvres of his uncle, a staunch supporter and favourite of Queen Elizabeth, who in 1597 appointed Ormond lieutenant-general of the army in Ireland (he had been Treasurer of Ireland since 1559). Ormond's influence led to Walter being knighted in January 1598-99 (despite a policy of the parsimonious Queen which demanded that Dublin be abstemious in its creation of knights).[106] Sir Walter appears to have worked hard to deserve his position as we read of his commanding a troop of fifty horsemen in 1598 when Black Tom set out to subdue rebels in Munster.[107]

In September 1599 the ill-fated Earl of Essex abandoned his post as Lord Lieutenant of Ireland to return to London. Soon after, Hugh O'Neill (the Earl of Tyrone), rose up, once again throwing Ireland – particularly Munster – into chaos. In the fighting which followed, Earl Thomas, accompanied by his nephew – who met O'Neill on Thomas's behalf on a number of occasions[108] – mustered men for the Queen. In 1600 Redmond Bourke threatened Butler land in Ormond, and Walter and his relative Lord Dunboyne were dispatched in command of a force of men to engage him. Walter and Dunboyne fell upon Bourke's soldiers early one morning and completely routed them, leaving their enemies as the *Annals of the Four Masters* put it, 'lying mangled and slaughtered, pierced and blood-stained corpses, throughout their tents and booths'.[109] During this conflict Walter was wounded in the knee.[110] Despite this though, he was back in battle before the close of the year defending his uncle's property in Kilkenny.[111]

Walter became one of two MPs for Tipperary in 1613-14. In parliament he was a leader of the Old English opposition to increased Anglicisation. He was one of the recusants who objected to the King's nomination of Sir John Davies as Speaker of the Irish Parliament, instead seating one of the Ormond feoffees in the Speaker's chair.[112] In April 1615, his uncle, the eighty-two year old Black Tom – now blind and increasingly senile – died. His two sons had predeceased him and his daughter had no children. Consequently, the politically 'awkward' and Catholic Walter succeeded as the 11th Earl of Ormond, much to the displeasure of King James.[113] Though Walter did not succeed to his uncle's positions as Lord High Treasurer or Vice-admiral of Leinster he was nonetheless one of the most powerful men in Ireland and a potential thorn in the side of the Dublin administration.[114]

It is as well to have noted Walter's early military career before going on to look at his private life and subsequent history. His piety earned him the nickname of 'Walter of the beads and the rosaries' and it is instructive to remember that this did not preclude the exercise of his skill in martial affairs. Walter married Ellen Butler (d. 1632), the eldest daughter of Edmond, 2nd Viscount Mountgarret, and they had two sons and nine daughters. The younger of the sons, James, died early and the other son, Thomas, Viscount Thurles, displeased his father by marrying without his permission.

Why Walter objected to his son's marriage to Elizabeth Poyntz (the daughter of a noble Catholic family from Gloucestershire) we do not know. Thomas and his wife had to spend the early years of their marriage in his father-in-law's house in London as they could not appear at Walter's household at Kilcash. Here, in England, Thomas's son James was born in 1610 and shortly afterwards Thomas and his wife came to Ireland to stay with the ageing Black Tom at Carrick, leaving their son to be nursed by a carpenter's wife at Hatfield.[115] In 1613 young James was brought to Carrick[116] where an apocryphal story about the child and the Old Earl refers to him as 'Jemmy Butler of Kilcash',[117] though, as we have seen, he never resided there. When in December of 1619 his father Viscount Thurles drowned off Skerries on his way to England (to answer charges of having garrisoned Kilkenny)[118] James became Walter's heir and so was made a ward of Court. He was brought up in the household of Archbishop Abbot of Canterbury to wean him from the troublesome Catholic influence of his family. James, who remained both a staunch Protestant and a Royalist – was to succeed to the Earldom on Walter's death and he was eventually created Marquess (1642) and later 1st Duke of Ormonde (1661).[119]

Another marriage caused further distress to Earl Walter. His first cousin Elizabeth, Black Tom's daughter, had married for a second time in 1614 just before her father's death. In part, this was Walter's own doing as he had hoped that Elizabeth's remarriage would relieve him of the responsibility of her first husband's debts.[120] In part it was also the fault of King James I who, as was his wont, married off Elizabeth to a favourite of his (one of the gentlemen of the Royal Bedchamber), Sir

Richard Preston. This marriage was to prove disastrous for Walter as Preston claimed the Ormond estates through his wife and the case eventually went to the King to be adjudicated, with a bond of £100,000 sterling being put up by both parties to enforce observance of the royal decision.[121]

Long years of service by the Catholic Earl to his Protestant sovereigns went unrewarded. King James decided that the Ormond estates should be divided with a large part (including Kilkenny) being awarded to Elizabeth and Preston. Earl Walter was outraged and refused to agree to the settlement. For his obstinacy he was arrested in June 1617 and committed to the Fleet prison in London. Here he remained until March 1625, living in conditions of abject poverty as the revenues of his estates were denied him. His imprisonment suited not only King James, but also the authorities in Dublin Castle who wished to reduce the Catholic Ormond influence in Munster.[122]

The years that Walter spent in prison were bitter ones. The Ormond liberty of Tipperary was abolished in 1620-21 and the family's hereditary right to the prisage of wines was revoked.* Preston was created Baron Dunmore and Earl of Desmond.[123] In the light of the old Ormond-Desmond feud, the revival of the latter title would really have rankled Walter. Worse was to come in the 1620s. In December 1621 a warrant was issued which conferred the wardship of Walter's grandson James on Preston (now Desmond). Along with this went the lease of Kilcash. For one reason or another the execution of the warrant was delayed but it was eventually enrolled in May 1623. To add to Walter's misfortune, one Piers Butler also appeared on the scene claiming that he was the rightful heir to the Earldom. Piers's claim was eventually rejected by a Royal Commission, but pending this judgement, the impotent and imprisoned Walter must have worried that his enemies were free to gain the upper hand.[124]

Eventually though, after the death of James I and the accession of his son Charles, Walter capitulated and accepted the royal settlement. He was immediately released and restored to the greater part of his lands. This allowed him to live for a while in London (in Drury Lane) with his grandson, James. Afterwards, both the Earl and James moved back to Ireland where they lived at Carrick-on-Suir.[125]

Towards the end of his life Walter enjoyed no respite from the cares that devolved on the head of the Butler family, as he had to battle with the encroachment of the Plantation of Munster on his

---

*The prisage of wines was a tax on all wines entering the country. It was subsequently recovered by the first Duke of Ormonde.

lands in Upper and Lower Ormond.[126] He may, however, have derived some satisfaction from the fact of outliving his cousin Elizabeth who died early in October 1628 and her – to Walter – ever troublesome husband who drowned when his ship sank later that same month.[127] He would also have forseen the reunification of the Ormond estates as after these deaths Walter's grandson and heir, James, began a 'vigorous but clandestine courtship'[128] of his cousin, the Prestons' daughter Elizabeth. After complex negotiations (and the payment of £15,000 to Elizabeth's guardian, the Earl of Holland), the two were eventually married in September 1629.[129] Walter himself died in Carrick in February 1632-3 and was laid to rest with his forebears in St Canice's Cathedral, Kilkenny.[130]

Richard Butler of Kilcash (c. 1616-1701)

Walter's son Thomas had two other sons in addition to James. His second son, John, died unmarried in Naples in 1636 while his youngest son, Richard, inherited Kilcash. As we have seen, Walter spent much of his life away from his home, having lived for long periods elsewhere. Richard, by contrast, was more often in residence, though during the Confederate Wars he was away on campaign and he underwent a brief exile during the Cromwellian period.

The life of James the 1st Duke of Ormonde has been treated of several times and at great length.[131] That of his brother Richard was scarcely less eventful though it was played out on a slightly less exalted stage. It is hardly surprising that a senior member of such a prominent Catholic family became caught up in the turmoil of mid-seventeenth century Ireland (a turmoil which was replicated in and connected to the English Civil Wars (1642-51) and the Thirty Years War in Europe (1618-48). It was a time when Irish Catholics, in part prompted by the 1641 rising in Ulster, banded together to assert their rights against the English. To this end the 'Confederate Catholics' (often called 'The Confederation of Kilkenny') formed in Kilkenny in 1642, an alliance in which the Butlers were deeply involved.

The rising of 1641 and its aftermath initially split the Butler family. James, Earl of Ormond and Richard's brother, was both a Protestant and a Royalist, acting as the lieutenant-general of King Charles's army in Ireland. Richard was the confederate governor of Waterford in command of 1200 infantry and 100 horsemen[132] and thus the brothers took to the field under opposing colours, eventually fighting on different sides of the battle of Kilrush, Co. Kildare (13 April 1642).[133] By early 1641-2 Richard had captured the towns of Carrick-on-Suir, Clonmel and Dungarvan. In a noteworthy victory he defeated a group of 1,500 Scots near Youghal.[134] In all his military successes he appears to have shown great restraint and gallantry. Lady Ormond, his sister in law, gathered with other Protestant English at Carrick was protected by him and facilitated in rejoining her husband[135] and some commentators note that thanks in part to Richard, the insurrection was not accompanied by the atrocities which were witnessed elsewhere.[136]

Burke records the handing over of the keys of Clonmel by the then mayor, John White, to Richard. One of the confederates' first actions was to return the town's churches to the Catholics.[137] This was in keeping with the character of a man who was later described by Bishop John Brennan as 'the most zealous Catholic…[who] has always been a protector of the clergy'.[138] Considering his position then, it is no surprise to learn that it was Richard who was sent by the Confederates to meet the papal legate, Archbishop Rinuccini (1592-1653) on his landing in Ireland.[139]

Richard's fortunes in war were soon to alter. A letter of 1642 records that Richard, along with over fifty others, had been taken by Murrough O'Brien, 1st Earl of Inchiquin and governor of Munster. This must have been one of the lowest points in Richard's career as all of his fellow officers, except one, were hanged shortly afterwards.[140] Richard, considered an important prisoner and a possible source of intelligence, was taken to Cork where he was held under close guard. By his own contrivance however, and to Inchiquin's evident embarrassment, the Colonel managed to escape, and rejoin the conflict.[141]

The Civil War in England made it necessary for Charles I to reconcile himself to his Catholic subjects in Ireland with the greatest possible speed. To this end, in the light of his loyalty and his extensive Catholic connections, Ormonde was appointed Lord Lieutenant of Ireland in January 1644. The ensuing history of the splits and factions is a complicated one as Catholics were divided on the matter of how they should treat the king's overtures. For us though, what is important is that Ormonde and Richard ended up making common cause against the parliamentarians. Early in 1647 a disguised Richard (with his wife's brother, the 3rd Earl of Castlehaven),[142] set out from the port of Waterford for France on the business of this new alliance. However, their ship encountered contrary winds and was forced back into the harbour where both Richard and Castlehaven were taken prisoner.[143]

Richard was freed or escaped sometime soon after, as later in 1647 we read of him in Rouen.[144] In August of 1649 Richard fought under the command of his brother, in the battle of Rathmines where the Royalist forces were pitted against the parliamentary Dublin garrison. In the affray Richard and his troops behaved bravely. All of Ormonde's left wing except the two regiments under the command of Richard and a

Colonel Miles Reilly broke and fled at the onslaught of the parliamentary forces.[145] Richard was wounded and once again captured (this time by a Colonel Raynolds).[146] The King's forces were defeated. At this stage Ormonde began to lose faith in achieving victory and, as a result, he eventually quit Ireland in December 1650.[147]

What happens to Richard at this point is difficult to determine exactly. The Carte papers record negotiations between Ormonde and Cromwell about his release.[148] There is also a surviving pass, signed by Cromwell in April of 1650, allowing Richard to go and see Ormonde on the provision that once he has transacted certain business with him, that he return. After this, it seems, he was to be released.[149] In any event, Richard somehow regained his freedom and in 1650, he, like his brother, went into exile until the Restoration of Charles II in 1660.[150]

In Richard's absence things went badly in Kilcash. Tipperary was preparing for the onslaught of Cromwell's army and in 1649 a garrison of 100 soldiers was sent from Clonmel (though it seems that this may have been intended more as a means of relieving overcrowding and tensions in the town than as a strategic measure).[151] A muster roll of January of the following year shows that soldiers were still present at Kilcash.[152] We do not know whether this garrison remained at Kilcash or whether they withdrew to Clonmel (where Cromwell's men breached the walls in May 1650 only to be trapped by the town's defenders). It has been suggested that the retreating garrison burned the tower house before they quit it.[153] It is of course also possible that the destruction of a fortification in hostile territory was the work of Cromwell's troops. What we are sure of is that the tower was taken by Cromwell's forces.[154] The *Civil Survey* (c. 1655) records that it suffered the fate of so many similar buildings in the 1650s, the period which witnessed the greatest destruction of tower houses.[155] The *Survey* notes 'the Castle and house of Killkash the walls only standing' and 'a castle and dwelling-house the roofe and lofts whereof are burnt and a Bawne with divers thatcht cabbins and a little church roofed'.[156]

Under the Cromwellian regime Richard naturally lost his lands. Kilcash was granted to an Englishman named John Blackwell.[157] Blackwell never lived in Kilcash and Richard's wife, Frances Butler (née Touchet) is recorded in the 1659 census as remaining there while her husband was on the Continent.[158]

These must have been arduous years for Lady Butler whose husband and brother were so embroiled in the wars that eventually forced both of them into exile.[159] Despite this we have evidence for her hospitality. Some refugees of prominent families from the opposing side of the conflict note that they were 'most nobly & kindly' received by Frances who kept them two days and two nights and would not suffer them to depart until she had found them safe lodgings in Carrick-on-Suir.[160] During the wars, the occasional visits paid to Kilcash by her soldier brother or husband were doubtless sources of relief in what were otherwise tense and anxious years.[161] In 1647 Richard writes to his brother Ormonde from Rouen.[162] He entreats 'your care of my wife, who I have left in great distraction and I hear since my coming [to France] is very much troubled'.[163]

The little we know of her life would seem to indicate that Frances was no stranger to difficulty, despite the fact that she came from a wealthy background (in 1636 her brother Castlehaven settled £2000 on her for her marriage portion).[164] Her early life was overshadowed by the infamy of her father which split her family. Her mother, Elizabeth Barnham, died young and her father, Mervyn Touchet, 2nd Earl of Castlehaven, remarried in 1624. This second marriage – to Anne, the widow of Grey Brydges, Baron of Chandos and Sudeley – was an unhappy one. Her father (and perhaps her step-mother) appear to have had an irregular sexual life. He was eventually arrested on two counts of sodomising a servant Laurence FitzPatrick, gay sex being at the time a crime in English civil law.[165] He was also charged with holding down his wife as she was raped by another one of his servants.[166] Having been found guilty of all charges he was attainted and beheaded on Tower Hill in London in May 1631. During the course of the trial a picture emerged of a lewd and depraved lifestyle. The Earl regularly molested his servants and encouraged one of them to have sexual relations both with his second wife and with his twelve year old step-daughter.[167] The events surrounding the senior Castlehaven's trial were the greatest scandals of the England of his day. What effect all of this can have had on the young Frances Touchet, we can only imagine. She must have been happy to escape in some measure from her past by marrying Richard.[168]

After Richard went into exile Lady Frances was thrown back on her own resources. In March 1660 she had to write to Lord Orory [sic] thanking him for looking after one of her sons. She would not, she says, have imposed on the lord's hospitality if it were not for the urgency of her 'present wants'.[169] After all, she had a sizeable family to look after; at least three sons that we know of (Walter, John and Thomas) and four daughters (Lucia, Mary, Frances and Elizabeth).[170] When her husband lost possession of Kilcash she was forced to appeal to Cromwell for financial assistance. In August of 1655 the Protector granted her 'a competent part of her jointure for the maintenance of herself and her children – or else £200 a year'.[171] This arrangement was soon changed however, and in place of the annual £200 the Council granted her a farm and some lands in Ballintubber in Connaught.[172] At the time the return on the farm was a mere £24 a year and we know that Lady Butler appealed the Council's decision, though the eventual outcome of her suit is not recorded.

Like her husband – and her brother George (d. 1689) who was a Benedictine – Lady Frances appears to have been a devout Catholic and in 1654 one Rev. Paul of St Ubald, of the reformed Order of Mary of Mount Carmel, dedicated a manual of mental prayer to her.[173] Under the circumstances, Paul of St Ubald could hardly have been hoping for patronage and Lady Frances Butler was not a figure of international celebrity, so we can read his dedication with some assurance that it is an authentic and sincere assessment, rather than an empty exercise in flattery.

Paul explained that the dedication arose from his 'reflecting on the piety and devotion, which in your, ladiship I observed being at Kilkash'[174] and his consideration of the 'great content which you [Lady Butler] took in speaking, and conversing of spirituall matters'.[175] His remembrances provide us with a glance at her life as he recalls 'the orderly composition of your chappell, with those devout pictures of the Altar, decent vestments, fine and clean Altar clothes, the observance of the houres for prayer'.[176] This seems to be the picture of a genuinely devout household.

Unfortunately, this glimpse of life at Kilcash – though valuable – is all too brief. In keeping with the fashion of the time, Paul expounds his method of prayer by employing figurative language such as that which gives the title to his sixth chapter: 'The Garden of the Soul'.[177] It is bearing this caveat in mind that we wonder whether or not some of this spiritual imagery was prompted by more secular memories of Kilcash. When he speaks of walking 'in every sort of prayer here laid downe for each state of life, as in the alleyes of a pleasant garden',[178] could he be drawing on the experience of his stay in Tipperary? Likewise, though once more it must be said that it is a conventional enough image, we wonder if there is recollection mingled in his description of his prayer manual as 'a table before you, with many diversityes of banqueting stuff, and dishes of rare, and comfortable meates'?[179] Though speculative, such passages capture the imagination of the reader and they provide us with a view of some of the pleasures of lives whose turbulent aspects are more usually recorded.

With the Restoration of the monarchy in England, Butler fortunes were reinstated. While in exile, Ormonde was one of the principal confidants of Charles II. It was Ormonde who oversaw the Irish Restoration land settlement, a settlement from which he and his family benefited not a little. There was a complication in restoring Richard to

Kilcash, as Richard had been a confederate rebel opposing Charles I before joining forces with the King 'against the tyrant Oliver'.[180] This problem was circumvented with some legal ingenuity. Ormonde's lawyers asserted that Kilcash had never legally been conveyed to Walter Butler and thus it was not Richard's to forfeit for rebellion. Blackwell was simply deprived of his land and Kilcash was granted to Richard, for the first time as it were.[181] In addition Richard may have received a pension of £1000 from Charles II[182] and he was made an MP for Gowran in Co. Kilkenny in 1689.

In Richard's time the Kilcash estate went through many changes. Despite the destruction of the Cromwellian wars, he added significantly to his lands. He had a large house in Mullenkeagh, near Borrisokane (though it is doubtful that he ever lived there)[183] while he also held property in Ballylusky, Borrisokane (Tipperary N. R.) and Borris (Co. Carlow) as well as elsewhere.[184] Around Kilcash itself, it is estimated that he controlled about 8,000 acres[185] and in the environs of the tower house there would have been a manorial style village with 27 hearths which, it is likely, would have had a forge and perhaps milling facilities.[186] After the wars Richard evidently engaged in some rebuilding as the *Hearth Money Records* tax him for three fireplaces in 1665-7[187] and there is reference in 1677 to his 'mansion house of Kilcash'.[188]

During the thirty years following the Restoration Richard seems to have enjoyed some of the fruits of his long battles. Kilcash became the 'fulcrum of the Catholic Butler dynasty of County Tipperary'[189] and it is noted that 'his palace has always been a sanctuary and refuge for ecclesiastics'.[190] His wife's brother, the Earl of Castlehaven, came to stay with them for a while and he may have revised his controversial *Memoirs* of the recent wars there. Unfortunately however, Richard's erstwhile comrade in arms died suddenly at Kilcash on October 11th 1684.[191]

In the final decades of his life the ageing Richard was to live through further personal and political griefs. Inevitably, he was of an age when his contemporaries were passing away and he most probably buried his wife, but he hardly expected to outlive his eldest son who died a year before he himself did in 1701. He also lived to see the Williamite War (1689-1691) and the enactment of the first penal laws. As the eighteenth century ended there was to be little peace for the family of Kilcash.

The Church in Kilcash between the Reformation and the Eighteenth Century

After the Reformation took effect the old church was no longer available for Catholic worship. What exactly replaced it is impossible to say. Mass houses, huts and portable altars are recorded in use all over Ireland throughout the succeeding centuries. During the time of Richard Butler and Lady Frances Touchet the *Civil Survey* records 'a Bawne with divers thatcht cabbins and a little church roofed'.[195] It may be, therefore, that the castle had a small church in its grounds the remains of which do not survive. This would be in keeping with the devotion and the status of the family resident in the castle while also fitting in with the picture of prayer which we saw painted by Paul of St Ubald.

In 1540 what had been the Catholic church land in the parish – specifically referred to as having been formerly in the possession of the Hospital – was leased to one John White for 13s 4d. It was valued at 20s.[193] Later in the Tudor period, under Queen Elizabeth, there are further records of leases on the land (which once again was noted as having been the property of the Hospital).[194] Towards the end of the reign of James I (1622) the rectory was rented for 1*l*.[195]

Just before this, in 1615, the church is described as having the 'chauncell repaired', with 'the boddy of the church decaied'. The parish of Kilcash was 'united by the Kinges pattent to Kilshillan' and the vicar of the united parish is listed as Jo. Gwyn, who also had the care of 'Tibraghny' and 'Taheny' (presumably the modern Tybroughney, Co. Kilkenny and Ahenny, Co. Tipperary). At the time the living yielded six Irish pounds to the Rev. Gwyn for which remuneration he 'some tymes' attended the Kilcash side of the parish. To put things in perspective it is worth noting that his attendance in Kilsheelan (where the church was 'somewhat in decay' and the living was worth twenty pounds) was just as sporadic. Rev. Gwyn complained that he could not find a curate to assist him with the result that at Taheny it was noted that 'the cure [was] not attended, but seldome by himselfe'.[196]

Somewhat later in the century, in 1640, the tithes of the church were held by an English Protestant called Medhopp who lived in King's County (Offaly). Our records for the period are not as detailed, but the church is listed as having two fenced-in plantation acres of land – valued at £2 – which were somewhere to the north of the church building, between it and Slievenamon.[197]

Of course the fact that the church was in Protestant hands did not prevent the Catholics from practising their faith and despite anti-Catholic legislation, throughout the seventeenth and eighteenth centuries the castle welcomed a host of Catholic clergy. Indeed, the Reformation was slow to take hold in Ireland, especially outside the Pale where the various acts establishing the Church of Ireland were difficult to enforce. In 1592 the first Irish College to train priests was opened in Salamanca in Spain, an event which marked the progress of the Irish Catholic Counter Reformation.

1588 was a particularly troubled year for Catholic-Protestant relations. It was the year of the Spanish Armada, a Papal-backed attack on an England governed by a queen who had been excommunicated since 1570. The Armada understandably became the source of a great deal of Protestant propaganda and heightened fears of Spanish/Catholic intervention in Irish affairs. It is in this light that we must understand the activity of the Protestant Ecclesiastical Commissions, bodies established to ensure that the Elizabethan church in Ireland was following the dictates of Protestant orthodoxy.

In 1588 a Commission records the presence of Rev. Thomas Geoffrey at Kilcash. He had evidently been practising under the new dispensation while remaining a Roman Catholic priest. The report of the Commission notes that he is 'a papist' and 'extremely contumacious'. As, in their eyes, his pastoral duties were carried out with 'notorious irregularity' he was suspended and the revenues of the living were sequestered.[198] This was not the end of the Rev. Geoffrey though. The 'Kilcash Chalice' with its Latin inscription 'Thomas Geoffrie the priest had me made in 1599'[199] is to-day in the possession of the Friary in Clonmel (it may have come to the Franciscans when Fr Richard Hogan, a member of their order, was a priest in Kilcash in the first half of the eighteenth century).[200] Geoffrey was still in Kilcash in the first decade of the seventeenth century. His presence, evidently concealed, was reported by a spy in 1604.[201] The contumacious Catholics would prove difficult to dispose of.

Another Kilcash chalice records the presence of a priest in the early seventeenth century. This chalice, which bears the Latin inscription 'Pray for the soul of Pa[trick?] Purcell, priest, who had me made, 1631' is unsurprising evidence that at the end of Walter Butler's time there were Catholic clergy active in the area.[202] We have already read of the visit later in the seventeenth century of Rev. Paul of St Ubald when Richard Butler was at Kilcash, in whose time the castle also sheltered Dr James Phelan the Bishop of Ossory (1621-1695), who was chaplain to the Butlers for eight years and who ordained priests at the castle in 1670 and 1671.[203] One of these, Peter Fonegal was ordained in 1671 and he later became Parish Priest of Thomastown in Kilkenny.[204]

Kilcash also opened its doors to Dr John Brenan, Archbishop of Cashel (d. 1693) and it was from the castle that he wrote his reports to Rome.[205] It was ultimately through this Archbishop that the arm-bone of Saint Oliver Plunkett (1625-81),[206] came to be kept at Kilcash as it was deposited there in the following century by some of the Butler Archbishops. Brenan had, it seems, been a fellow student and friend of Plunkett's. How exactly he came to possess the arm-bone is not known, but it seems that after Plunkett was executed both of his arms, to the elbows were 'reverently detached by a surgeon'.[207] In 1872 this relic passed into the keeping of the Dominican Convent in Cabra (Dublin) who still have it in their care.[208]

References

1. W. P. Burke (1894-5), 266. He also mentions Colman of Kilcash in William Burke (1983/1907), 3.
2. 'Díarmaid Cille Caisi décc'. John O'Donovan ed. (1636/1990), I, 475 (orthography modernised). The 'falling asleep' of 'Diarmait of Cill-Can' is recorded in the *Annals of Ulster* for the year 847. Scholars have thought that 'Cill-Can' is 'Cill Caisi'. [William M Hennessy et al eds. (1887-1901), I, 365]. However for a recent assessment of this see Pádraig Ó Cearbhall (1993) and his PhD thesis (a draft of which he has kindly sent us) to be submitted in UCD in 1999.
3. It is however, identified as such by Ed. Hogan (1910), 180.
4. 'Item campus del Schur usque Kilcaxe continet lxvj acras'. [Newport B. White ed. (1932), 55]. White lists this Kilcaxe under Kilcash in his index. Sixty six medieval acres would equate to approximately 165 statute acres.
5. We are grateful to Canon C. A. Empey for suggesting this to us.
6. Pádraig Ó Cearbhaill (1993) provides an extensive discussion of the exact form of the name. In ibid., 89-90 there is a near exhaustive list of the Latin and English variants of 'Kilcash', while an equally thorough list of Irish forms can be found at ibid., 94.
7. For Kilkeasy/*Cill-Caisi* see John Francis Shearman (1879), 316.
8. John O'Donovan (1930/1840), 54; P. Power (1952), 265.
9. John O'Donovan trans. (1864/1630), 111.
10. John Francis Shearman (1879), 315.
11. Pádraig Ó Rian ed. (1985), 178.
12. We are grateful to Pádraig Ó Cearbhall of the Place-names section of the Ordnance Survey Office for showing us a draft of his PhD thesis on the place-names of Tipperary to be submitted to UCD in 1999. See also his article of 1993.
13. Con Manning (1995), 14.
14. Ibid., 5.
15. B. J. Graham (1993a), 23.
16. P. D. Sweetman (1984), 36.
17. Conversation with Con Manning, Senior Archaeologist, Dúchas. See chapter I for more detail.
18. The *Register* records Baldwin's gift as two carucates. My calculation presumes that there were 120 medieval acres in a carucate with one medieval acre corresponding to roughly $2^1/_2$ statute acres. [See Mark Hennessey (1988), 42].
19. Eric St John Brooks (1936), 294.
20. Ibid., 296.
21. Butler influence becomes marked in the fourteenth century with the creation of the title of Earl of Ormond and the Liberty of Tipperary in 1329. The systems of alliances and marriages arranged by James the 3rd Earl and his son the 5th Earl (The 'White Earl') represents the summit of Butler power in the medieval period. [See C. A. Empey, 'Ormond (Butler) in S. J. Connolly ed. (1998), 416-7].
22. Thereby advantage could be taken of existing resources, population distribution and the geographical advantages which determined pre-existing settlements. See the references in B. J. Graham (1993b), 67.

23. See C. A. Empey, 'cantred' and 'manor' in S. J. Connolly ed. (1998), 69 and 343-4.
24. Mark Hennessey (1985), 61. C. A. Empey (1983), 451.
25. W. H. Bliss ed. (1893), 370.
26. See C. A. Empey (1982), 334. Judging from Baldwin's largesse in respect of his donation to the Hospital, from the presence of the church and from its position, Kilcash is likely to have been a manor. However, the paucity of sources does not allow us to be certain on this point. The *Civil Survey* (1640) (R. C. Simington ed. (1931), 271) notes that Kilcash 'is and was anciently held a manor. in free and Com[m]on soccage from the Earls of Ormond with Court-leet and Court Barron and severall other privileges'.
27. See B. J. Graham (1993b), 74.
28. Eric St John Brooks (1936), 294. Our translation from the Latin.
29. For Richard de Valle see Hubert Gallwey (1970), 187 who claims (wrongly, as it seems to us) that Richard is the founder of the manor of Kilcash.
30. C. A. Empey (1985), 73.
31. See C. A. Empey (1970), 4.
32. Ibid., 5-6.
33. Ibid., 16, 18. This information is also summarised in Count de la Poer (1898), 116-119.
34. Edmund Curtis ed. (1932-43), II, no. 49. These records survive in the Ormond papers as the Earl, after the establishment of the Liberty (later called the Palatinate) of Tipperary, had legal control of all non church lands unless the crime were reserved to the Crown (as in the case of arson or rape). [See C. A. Empey (1985), 75, 89].
35. Edmund Curtis ed. (1932-43), II, no. 361. That the victim of the crime was a Wall is an indication that the Kilcash referred to was indeed the Old Kilcash with which we are dealing.
36. Conrad Cairns (1994), I, 47.
37. Edmund Curtis ed. (1932-43), V, no. 1. Both incidents took place c. 1548.
38. H. S. Sweetman (1886), 307. The record refers to 1302.
39. Hubert Gallwey (1970), 187.
40. Norman Cohn [(1975), 203] represents Alice's trial as an important step in the formation of the popular notion of the witch. As Keith Thomas [(1991), 528] notes, the Kyteler case was one of only three involving charges of deliberate devil-worship. Before this time witchcraft was considered a petty crime where it was the subject of small fines rather than capital punishment.
41. A contemporary Latin record of the case can be found in Thomas Wright's (1843) *Narrative of the Proceedings against Dame Alice Kyteler for sorcery*. This is summarised in St John D. Seymour (1989/1913) and later translated into English by L. S Davidson & J. O. Ward in 1993 [see bibliography]. Less reliable, derivative sources can be found in J. T. Gilbert ed. (1884). *Chartularies of St Mary's Abbey, Dublin*. Vol 2. London: Rolls Series and in Holinshed's *Chronicle of Ireland*. London, 1587 [See Norman Cohn (1975), 286 n. 39]. There are also brief mentions of Kyteler in other contemporary sources such as the Close Rolls and Patent Rolls. For the most part these are collected and translated in L. S. Davidson and J. O. Ward eds. (1993).
42. W. B. Yeats (1992), 256. From the detail, it seems to us that Yeats is working from the account in Holinshed.
43. Chaucer (1990), 105.
44. As Dr Bernadette Williams has pointed out to us in conversation, the supposition that this man was called William has no foundation in any of the primary

sources. It derives from an error in Wright ed. (1843), 60-1.
45. Bernadette Williams (1999). We are grateful to Dr Williams for showing a manuscript of her forthcoming article to us. As it has not been published yet we have not provided any page references.
46. Ibid.
47. Hubert Gallwey (1970), 188. A widow was entitled to the revenue from a third of her deceased husband's estates for the duration of her life.
48. Bernadette Williams (1999) believes that Alice may in fact have poisoned some of her husbands. The medical symptoms of le Poer are similar to those which would result from the ingestion of a variety of substances available in the middle ages including gold, arsenic, thallium and selenium. However, it may be better to be wary of making a medical diagnosis on such scant evidence and the scant detail of the case which survives could also be in keeping with a variety of immune deficiency states or hyperthyroidism.
49. Thomas Wright (1843), 2. Occasionally we prefer our own translation to that of Davidson and Ward. In such cases reference is made to the Latin text in Wright.
50. c. 1302 William Outlawe is recorded as having in his safe-keeping £3,000 belonging to Alice and Adam le Blund. A measure of what this was worth is indicated by the fact that the average labourer of the day earned between 1 d and 1½d. [Bernadette Williams (1999)].
51. For brief biographies of the Bishop see *The Dictionary of National Biography* and Anne Neary (1984).
52. Norman Cohn (1975), 202.
53. Bernadette Williams (1999)
54. The fact that he bothered to personally instigate a visitation of his diocese (the visitation which turned up the accusations against Alice) was a sign of his commitment. [L. S. Davidson & J. O. Ward eds. (1993), 26, n.3].
55. Anne Neary (1984), 275.
56. L. S. Davidson & J. O. Ward eds. (1993), 28.
57. 'Incubus' is appropriately derived from the Latin 'one who lies upon'.
58. L. S. Davidson & J. O. Ward eds. (1993), 30.
59. Norman Cohn (1975), 200.
60. Ibid., 201.
61. L. S. Davidson & J. O. Ward eds. (1993), 31.
62. The decree *Si quis suadente* of the Second Latern Council (1139) anathematised any person daring to lay 'violent hands on a cleric or a monk'. Such an offence could, in the ordinary course of events, only to be forgiven by the Pope. [The decree is translated in L. S. Davidson & J. O. Ward eds. (1993), 71].
63. Anne Neary (1984), 278. Norman Cohn (1975), 202.
64. According to the contemporary *Annales Hiberniae* of Friar John Clyn. [Translated in L. S. Davidson & J. O. Ward eds. (1993), 80]. The *Narrative* records that unnamed others of Alice's 'pestiferous society' were burnt, excommunicated, whipped or exiled. [L. S. Davidson & J. O. Ward eds. (1993), 70].
65. Bernadette Williams (1999) believes that Alice was en route to her ancestral home in Flanders when she died in England. A legend about a witch called Alice Kettle with a familiar called Robert Artisson survives in the West Riding of Yorkshire which would have been part of Alice's itinerary were she crossing England to escape de Ledrede. We are grateful to Dr Williams for sharing the written account of the legend with us (for more information see the notes to her article). However, as the details of the legend coincide closely with the account of Alice Kettle's trial in Holinshed (down to the repetition of a spell/rhyme he

attributes to her), we feel that it is more likely that it was the result of a conflation of local mythology and the *Chronicle of Ireland*. [For a translation of the relevant passage in Holinshed see L. S. Davidson & J. O. Ward eds. (1993), 81-2].

66. The roof collapsed under the weight of the lead in a storm of 1332.
67. L. S. Davidson & J. O. Ward eds. (1993), 21.
68. Hubert Gallwey (1970), 190.
69. B. J. Graham (1993b), 76.
70. Hubert Gallwey (1970), 190.
71. Edmund Curtis ed. (1932-43), VI, no 5.
72. Ibid., IV, no 40.
73. Hubert Gallwey (1970), 192.
74. Edmund Curtis ed. (1932-43), V, no 1.
75. Hubert Butler (1970), 194, 196. See *The Irish Fiants of the Tudor Sovereigns* (1994), II, 126, 405.
76. Though often confused with the Knights Hospitallers, they were in fact a distinct order who were under the direct control of Rome rather then the local Ordinary (bishop).
77. See Aubrey Gwynn & R. Neville Hadcock (1970), 212 and Elizabeth Malcom, 'hospitals and dispensaries' in S. J. Connolly ed. (1998), 247.
78. Mark Hennessey (1985), 65-66 q.v.
79. Mark Hennessey (1988), 43.
80. Ibid., 49.
81. c. 1370-90 the parish appears in a roll of amercements on parishes of the diocese. See Newport B. White (1936), 230.
82. Aubrey Gwynn & R. Neville Hadcock (1970), 212.
83. Edmund Curtis ed. (1932-43), II, no 282.
84. Hubert Gallwey (1970), 191.
85. National Library of Ireland MS 2551. The date is uncertain as the manuscript uses both 1474 and 1478.
86. C. A. Empey and Katharine Simms (1975), 162.
87. Ibid., 178.
88. See C. A. Empey, 'Ormond (Butler)' in S. J. Connolly ed. (1998), 417. The Earls John and Thomas appear to have enjoyed some success in England though. Edward IV regarded John as 'the first gentleman in Christendom' and Thomas was raised to a peerage in England (in addition to his Irish title). [See Lord Dunboyne (1991), 12].
89. We are grateful to C. A. Empey for showing us his transcription of the *Statues* and discussing their nature with us.
90. Lecture, Ken Nicholls (UCC), Cahir, 25th February 1999.
91. W. G. Neely (1989), 33.
92. Patrick C. Power (1976), 34, 44 n. 24. James (d. Oct. 1546) made two wills which mention Kilcash. The first (1545) leaves it, along with various other lands, in the hands of various churchmen. This will was emended in March of 1546 to leave Kilcash to his son John. [See Edmund Curtis ed. (1932-43), IV, no 352].
93. T. B. Barry (1993), 114.
94. Edmund Curtis ed. (1932-43), IV, no 267.
95. Ibid., 329.
96. *The Irish Fiants of the Tudor Sovereigns* (1994), II, 13.
97. Hans Claude Hamilton ed. (1860), 227.
98. Ibid.

99. Edmund Curtis (1932-43), V, no. 150. Dated October 1567.
100. According to Hubert Butler. NLI MS 12024.
101. William F Butler (1929), 43-4.
102. See Thomas Carte (1851/1735-6), I, xlvi.
103. Thus Hubert Butler. NLI MS. 12024. See also Edmund Curtis, V, no. 139, a settlement on Sir Edmond Butler, dated 22 June 1564, which refers to the heirs male of John Butler of Kilcash (suggesting therefore that John is dead?).
104. Edmund Curtis ed. (1932-43), II, no 361. That the patronage of 'Kilconnell' was appendant to the manor of Kilcash was certified by the Archbishop of Cashel in June 1545 [Newport B. White (1936), 193-7 q.v.].
105. Patrick C. Power (1976), 45-6.
106. Ernest George Atkinson ed. (1895), 35.
107. Ibid., 323.
108. Ibid., 111, 114, 116, 117. There is evidence that, at about this time, there was a conspiracy on the part of some of Walter's men to have him killed and handed over to the rebels. [See ibid., 423].
109. John O'Donovan ed. (1636/1990), VI, 2227.
110. See Thomas Carte (1851/1735-6), I, cxi and Lady Burghclere (1912), I, 23. The *Dictionary of National Biography* gives the date of this skirmish as 1599.
111. See Thomas Carte (1851/1735-6), I, cxiv and the *Dictionary of National Biography*.
112. See Aileen McClintock (1988), 162; H. A. Doubleday and Lord Howard de Walden eds. (1911-40), X, 148 and Victor Treadwell (1998), 122.
113. Victor Treadwell (1998), 122.
114. Ibid., 123.
115. See J. C. Beckett (1990), 6-7.
116. Thomas Carte (1851/1735-6), I, 6.
117. Historical Manuscripts Commission (1895-1912), II, 347.
118. Lord Dunboyne (1991), 17. See also Thomas Carte (1851/1735-6), I, lxxi.
119. The 'e' is added to Ormond in the patent which created James Marquess of Ormonde in 1642 [See Lord Dunboyne (1991), 18, where the date is incorrectly given as 1652]. In consequence, 'Ormonde' is used here to refer to the family after this date.
120. Aileen McClintock (1988), 163. Victor Treadwell notes that Walter facilitated the marriage on behalf of the King to remain in royal favour. [(1998), 123].
121. Victor Treadwell (1998), 124.
122. Aileen McClintock (1988), 163.
123. Victor Treadwell (1998), 125-6.
124. Ibid., 128-9.
125. Thomas Carte (1851/1735-6), I, 17.
126. Aileen McClintock (1988), 166.
127. Victor Treadwell (1998), 296.
128. Ibid.
129. H. A. Doubleday and Lord Howard de Walden eds. (1911-40), IV, 367.
130. Thomas Carte (1851/1735-6), I, cxx.
131. See the biographies by Thomas Carte, Lady Burghclere and J. C. Beckett listed in the bibliography.
132. See the contemporary account by Bellings in J. T. Gilbert ed. (1882-1891), I, 71.
133. According to Hubert Butler [NLI MS. 12024].
134. Historical Manuscripts Commission (1906), 185.
135. See Belling's account in J. T. Gilbert ed. (1882-1891), I, 57 and Patrick C. Power

(1976), 48.
136. See Lady Burghclere l(1912), I, 160 and William Burke (1983/1907), 62. It is to be expected that this acclaim was not universal. See the deposition of Margaret Shaftoe who claims that she was robbed by Richard [TCD MS. 821/26].
137. William Burke (1983/1907), 62.
138. Bishop Brennan's reference is from 1692. Dermot F. Gleeson (1938), 119.
139. Thomas L. Coonan (1954), 205. Rinuccini, easily capable of being deprecating towards the Anglo-Irish Catholics, describes him as 'a good Catholic and a virtuous man' and as 'the most perfect of Catholics'. ['...optimum Catholicum et virum praeclarum'. 'Catholicus perfectissimus'. In John Kavanagh ed. (1932-1949), I, 642; II, 25].
140. James Hogan (1936), 149.
141. Ibid., 160. A letter from Inchiquin to England attempting to exonerate himself from any responsibility for Richard's escape.
142. Castlehaven (the title is from Co. Cork) though he does speak of Richard's military exploits [(1815), 57], does not mention this incident in his *Memoirs*. Even a cursory glance at his entry in the *Dictionary of National Biography* reveals Castlehaven's life (1617-84) to have been an unusual one from his earliest days. Born into a family notorious for sexual irregularity, he was married at Kilkenny in 1678/9 at the age of 13 or 14 to Elizabeth Brydges, a daughter of his father's second wife by her first husband. He spent his life as a soldier, joining the Irish wars on the side of the Confederates, for which he was indicted for high treason and imprisoned in 1642. He escaped to battle against Ormond, before going to France to fight under Prince Rupert (Charles II's cousin). He returned to Ireland to join Ormond against Cromwell. In 1652 Castlehaven, in common with many Irish Royalists, was forced into exile and he fought in France under Condé in the Fronde war (where he was again imprisoned). On his attaining his liberty in 1653 he entered Spanish service only returning to England after the Restoration where he fought in the Second Dutch War (1665). In 1674 he returned to war on the Continent again.
143. According to a letter written by Lord Inchiquin from Cork in March 1647. [Historical Manuscripts Commission (1905), 380-1].
144. See John Kavanagh ed. (1932-1949), II, 771.
145. J. T. Gilbert (1882-1891), VII, 128.
146. Lady Burghclere (1912), I, 367.
147. Hiram Morgan, 'Ormond, James Butler, 12th earl and 1st duke of' in S. J. Connolly ed. (1998), 418.
148. William Burke (1983/1907), 70n.
149. Historical Manuscripts Commission (1895-1912), I, 148.
150. Patrick C. Power (1976), 52.
151. William Burke (1983/1907), 67.
152. Ibid., 71n.
153. Patrick C. Power (1989), 70. See also Patrick C. Power (1976), 51.
154. Conrad Cairns (1994), I, 118.
155. Ibid., 70.
156. Robert C. Simington ed. (1931), 271.
157. Patrick C. Power [(1976), 54] claims that the grant was made to Blackwell in payment for his services in the execution of Charles I.
158. Séamas Pender ed. (1939), 310.
159. One of her sisters, Dorothy (d. 1634/5) was also married to a Confederate leader, Edmund Butler (d. 1679), the heir of Lord Mountgarret. Dorothy lived at Park's

Grove near Ballyragget in Co. Kilkenny. See H. A. Doubleday and Lord Howard de Walden eds. (1911-40), IX, 323.
160. TCD MS. 820/316b. The same deposition records Richard's generosity in the affair.
161. Her brother records his retiring to Kilcash for a rest in 1643 [Castlehaven (1815), 59].
162. Rinuccini records the visit. See John Kavanagh ed. (1932-1949), II, 771.
163. Historical Manuscripts Commission (1875-1912), I, 117.
164. NLI MS. D4007.
165. The unfortunate Fitzpatrick was executed on the strength of his evidence against the Earl. He had mistakenly thought that the evidence he provided in the Earl's trial could not have been used against him. [*Cobbet's Complete Collection of State Trials* (1809), 415f.].
166. *Cobbet's Complete Collection of State Trials* (1809), 401.
167. The rather shocking details of this latter fact emerged during the trial when the girl herself took the stand. [*Cobbet's Complete Collection of State Trials* (1809), 412].
168. The notion - fostered by Laurence Stone - that marriages were contracted by parents on the basis of property considerations which had no reference to the wishes of the couple has been greatly exaggerated. Though of course questions of money and rank were often significant to a prospective match, it would only be finalised if there were 'mutual liking' between the parties involved [See David Cressy (1997), 261].
169. NLI Ormond Papers 2325/91.
170. Hubert Butler. NLI MS. 12024.
171. Robert Pentland Mahaffy ed. (1903), 628.
172. Ibid., 629.
173. We know nothing about the life of Paul. The text mentions that his alias (his name before he joined the order) was 'S. B.'. Does the 'B' stand for Butler? Was he one of the scions of the family who joined the priesthood?
174. Paul of St Ubald (1654), A2r.
175. Ibid., A2v.
176. Ibid., A2r.
177. Ibid., 64.
178. Ibid., A4v.
179. Ibid.
180. The phrase is from a petition of Richard's to Charles II (3 November 1660) reminding the King of his loyal service both in Ireland and abroad. Richard was petitioning to have his lands restored and the 'adventurers and soldiers' who were then occupying them moved to Carlow or elsewhere [Robert Portland Mahaffy ed. (1905), 73].
181. Patrick C. Power (1976), 55.
182. Historical Manuscripts Commission (1875-1912), III, 398. It is impossible from the reference to tell whether the Richard in question is Richard of Kilcash. Tracing Richard's doings is complicated by the fact that there were two other Colonel Richard Butler's involved with the Confederates including a son of the 3rd Viscount Mountgarret.
183. Dermot F. Gleeson (1938), 200. Gleeson has 'Mullenreagh', but we presume that this is a misprint for Mullenkeagh in the Barony of Lower Ormond in the parish of Modreeny (near Borrisokane).
184. Ibid., 119.

185. William Smyth (1985), 113.
186. Ibid., 127, 445 n. 35 q.v.
187. Thomas Laffan ed. (1911), 30.
188. NLI MS. D4957. Dated 3 December 1677.
189. William Smyth (1985), 137.
190. Bishop Brennan in 1692 quoted in Dermot F. Gleeson (1938), 119.
191. P. Lynch (1815), xxvii.
192. Robert C. Simington ed. (1931), 271.
193. Newport B. White ed. (1943), 65.
194. *The Irish Fiants of the Tudor Sovereigns* (1994), II, 36, 621 q.v.
195. M. C. Griffith ed. (1966), 510.
196. TCD MS. 1066/286-7.
197. Robert C. Simington ed. (1931), 270.
198. W. P. Burke (1894-5), 310.
199. A later Latin inscription reads 'Father MA Holohan OSF of Waterford restored me in 1871'. This ornate chalice is 23.5 cm high standing on a hexagonal base chased with a band of small crosses. The cup is 10.1 cm in diameter and 7.6 cm deep.
200. W. P. Burke (1894-5), 310.
201. Patrick C. Power (1989), 60.
202. Patrick Power (1912), 149.
203. William Carrigan (1905), 319.
204. Patrick C. Power (1989), 85.
205. See James Maher (1954), 34 and James Maher (1969), 83.
206. Plunkett was Archbishop of Armagh. He was accused of aiding a plan for a French invasion. After a notoriously corrupt trial he was executed. He was canonised in 1975.
207. Monsignor Lyons (1937), 118. Plunkett's body had a history worthy of his involved life. His two arms, his head and his body travelled to various destinations in Europe before they found their current resting places [See ibid., *passim*].
208. See James Maher (1954), 35-6. We are grateful to Mrs. Una Power of Clonmel for information regarding the history of the relic.

Chapter III

The Eighteenth Century

Richard Butler's son, Colonel Walter Butler (d. 1700) was the first of the Butlers to live at Garryricken (near Windgap, Co. Kilkenny). Like his parents he appears to have been a devout Catholic, and Dr Phelan, the Bishop of Ossory ordained priests at his house on at least ten occasions between 1675 and 1688.[1] Walter had married Mary Plunkett, the only daughter of the 2nd Earl of Fingal and their eldest son, Thomas inherited Kilcash, while their third son,[2] Christopher (1673-1754), went on to become the Catholic Archbishop of Cashel, having been nominated for the position by James III (1688-1766), the 'old pretender'.[3]

Thomas Butler (d. 1738) and Margaret Burke, Viscountess Iveagh (d. 1744)

In the history of Kilcash, the eighteenth century opens with and is dominated by Thomas Butler and his wife, Margaret, Viscountess Iveagh. Little is recorded about Thomas's early life, though we do know that sometime prior to 1689 he had travelled as far as Hungary.[4] It is likely that he was there rallying to the call of the Holy Roman Empire in its fight against the Turks who besieged Vienna in 1683, but who were eventually repulsed and expelled from central and western Hungary after the siege of Buda (1686). Though we have no direct evidence of this, it would be following in the footsteps of the many Butlers who were in the Austrian service. (No fewer than six Butlers served as officers during the Thirty Years' war).[5] Thomas's fighting in Hungary would also have been in keeping with his Jacobite and Catholic affiliations. We know that the youthful James Fitzjames (1670-1734) – the illegitimate son of James II, created Duke of Berwick in 1637 – who would be Thomas's battalion commander during the Williamite wars was present at the siege of Buda, so perhaps they were acquainted before Berwick came to Ireland.

During the Irish Wars between the Protestant William III (1650-1702) and the Catholic James II (1633-1701), the Butlers of Kilcash had naturally sided with the Jacobites.[6] Thomas Butler was made an infantry

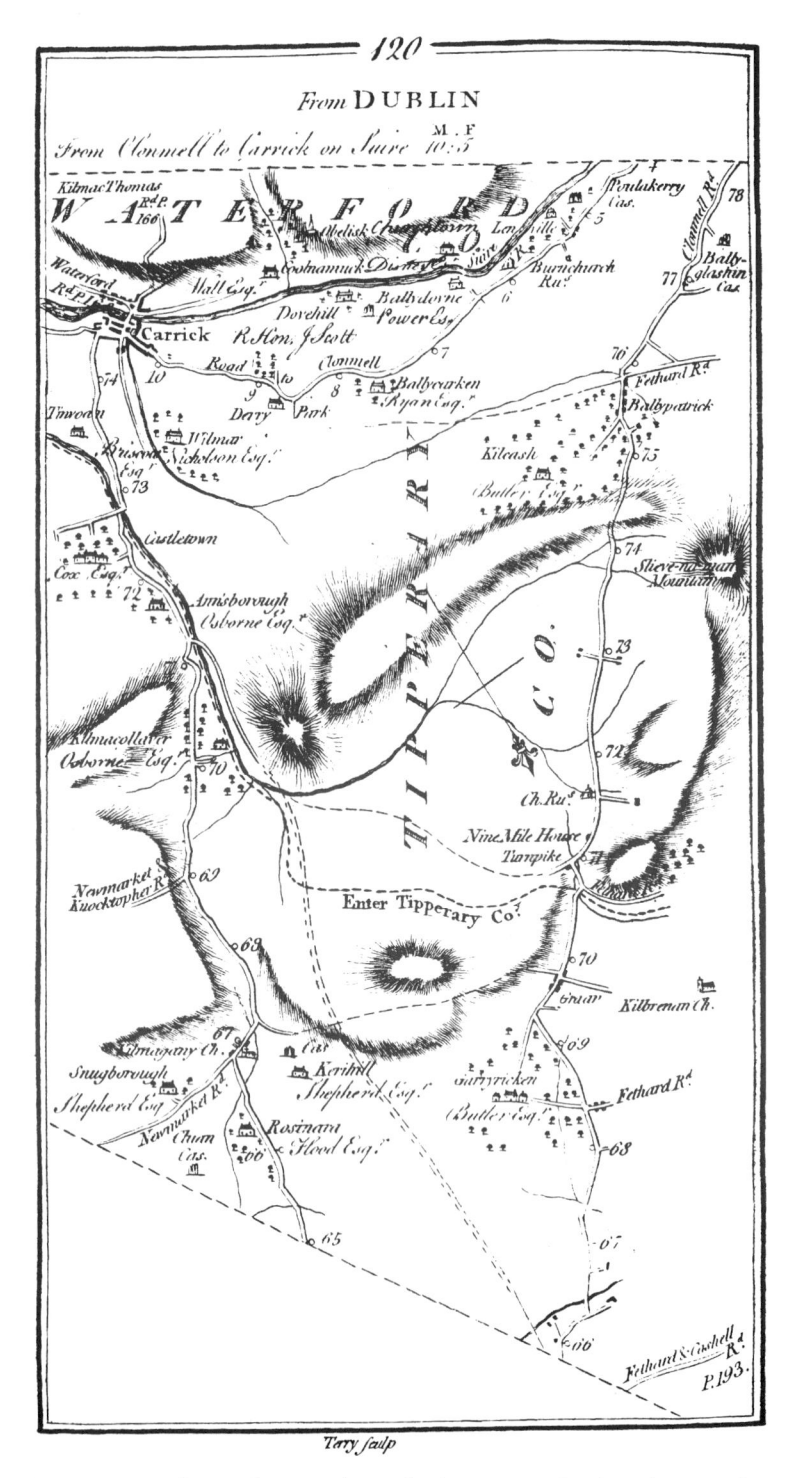

Illus. 3: A map of 1777 showing the Butler houses at Kilcash and Garryricken.

Plate 20: Thomas Butler of Kilcash.

colonel in the Jacobite army and he commanded a regiment which at one stage numbered 428 soldiers in addition to officers.[7] Some of Thomas's military fortunes and movements can be reconstructed. In July of 1689 orders came from the French officer Monsieur Rosen to the effect that Thomas was to reinforce the Duke of Berwick's troops.[8] Thus we find him in September at Drogheda in joint command of a battalion with the teenage Colonel Henry Fitzjames (b. 1673) – an illegitimate son of James II known as 'The Grand Prior' – which in turn was under the leadership of the Duke of Berwick and the Marquis

Descots.[9] At this stage Thomas had about four hundred men under his command[10] about half of whom were armed with good muskets while fifty-eight of them bore pikes.[11] The remainder seem to have had no arms worth speaking of, as many of the infantry were poor and therefore badly equipped for war. Initially however, the war went well for the Jacobites, and even after the defeat at the battle of the Boyne (July 1690) – which we presume that Thomas fought in – their position was still strong in Munster and Connaught.

The Williamite army in Ireland was reinforced by several thousand Danish troops hired to William by their king, Christian V. The Danish force was commanded by a German soldier, the Duke of Würtemberg-Neustadt. In October 1690 the Danes were involved in a battle against the Jacobites in Kinsale. The Jacobites were forced to retreat to their stronghold where, unfortunately for them, their ammunition exploded and in the resulting chaos many of them were captured, including Thomas Butler.

After this, Butler was either freed or he escaped as he was back with the Jacobites in Galway in early 1691. Würtemberg – on the strength of their earlier acquaintance from Thomas's visit to the Continent – wrote to him from Clonmel. In an effort to destabilise the Jacobite ranks the German Duke reassured Thomas of William III's good intentions towards the Irish. In a revealing passage which must reflect the Jacobite concerns, he promises that William would guarantee the Irish 'freedom of your religion and the security of your estates, together with the continuance of the rank or employment of those who would like to carry on a military career'. He also has a personal inducement for Thomas: 'for yourself in particular, I shall do my best to have you given the rank of brigadier'.[12]

Within a few days of receiving this letter Thomas wrote to Würtemberg thanking him for his solicitude. Unfortunately he felt that he could not help the Duke as though 'everyone here is agreed about the good intentions of King William', 'on the other hand we are quite unable to endure the yoke of the English, who after his death will not fail to break their word, so hostile are they to this nation'.[13] Thomas's loyalties were not to be bought, neither for military promotion nor out of concern for his grandfather Richard of Kilcash, who at the time was under Würtemberg's 'protection'.[14]

At about this juncture Thomas's regiment was down to three hundred men. Doubtless his troops had seen a lot of fighting and as men died or were wounded they would have been partially replaced by new recruits joining their fortunes with the Jacobite cause. Then, in July of 1691, the Jacobites lost the decisive battle of Aughrim (Co. Galway) to the Williamite General Ginkel. In the course of the fighting

Thomas had his horse shot out from under him and he was one of many officers taken prisoner.[15] In fact, Thomas was fortunate to have survived at all, as the total losses of the Jacobites on that bloody day exceeded 7,000 men and the Jacobite commander – the French Marquis de Saint-Ruth – was decapitated by a cannon ball at the outset of the combat.[16] When the remains of Thomas's battalion reassembled at Limerick there were 157 active soldiers armed with fifty-one working firearms and fourteen broken ones.[17] Nearly half their original number had been lost or wounded and their equipment was ruined. Thomas's days of war were over.

At this point Thomas Butler's relationship to the 2nd Duke of Ormonde proved very valuable to him. Through the agency of his cousin he was pardoned for his part in the battle of Aughrim and allowed to return to Kilcash.[18] Under a legal system which prevented Catholics from bearing arms, Colonel Butler was one of the few specially licensed to have in his possession a gun, a sword and a case of pistols. Considering his military history, this was no small concession on the part of the authorities and can only be accountable to family influence. Nonetheless, in times of civil unrest, such licences were occasionally suspended, as when in August 7th 1714 he had to hand up his weapons to the local Justice of the Peace, Richard Whitehead, the Protestant Mayor of Clonmel.[19]

Thomas's life at Kilcash, though peaceful after Aughrim, was not untroubled. He still maintained an interest in politics, and as late as 1725 he was one of the Jacobite sympathisers in Munster who possessed a code name.[20] The penal laws, which became increasingly rigorous in the early 1700s, prevented him from taking the place in social and political life which would otherwise have been his (amongst other things, the laws excluded Catholics from being MPs, practising law, holding office in local or national government and from service in the army). From an economic perspective the laws were also restrictive, affecting Catholics in their buying or inheriting of land. Though the degree of rigour with which they were enforced is a matter of controversy, recent historical work emphasises the fact that the principal victims of their restrictions were the remaining Catholic aristocracy and gentry.[21] Added to this, the late 1720s and early 1730s were lean and uncertain years for agriculture[22] and so in 1729 (a year of famine in Ireland) we find a somewhat embarrassed Thomas – 'being disabled by the gout' – writing through a secretary looking for the repayment of some money:

> Its a sensible trouble to me to hear how ill Coln Hamerlon is but do trust in God he will get the bettr [sic] of it. I shall also begg

pardon in desiting you will put him in mind of a small debt he owes me & put me in some way of payment wch shall be easy to him, tho' this debt be of long standing, yet I was unwilling to press him to it, and would so still but for some urgent occasion I have for it & forbore writing to himself for fear of giving him any disturbance.[23]

In the same vein, an undated letter to his son-in-law, Kenmare, forms part of a dispute which was going on about the size of his daughter's dowry.[24]

Visits from Thomas's brother Christopher, who had studied at the Sorbonne in Paris and had been consecrated Archbishop of Cashel in Rome in 1712,[25] must have been both occasions for anxiety as well as for hospitality. A law of William III's made it an act of treason for Catholic bishops to return to Ireland.[26] On May 6th 1713 a spy reported that the Archbishop had been staying at Kilcash during the previous six months. On May 27th, the High Sheriff conducted a search of the castle and grounds both for the Archbishop and for John Pierce the Bishop of Waterford, but he failed to find any trace that they had ever been there.[27] Christopher was a marked man and a permanent fugitive from the authorities and their professional priest hunters.[28] The subsequent public involvement of his cousin, the 2nd Duke, with the Jacobite cause made the Archbishop all the more suspect and it was even alleged that he was involved in a plot to help the pretender to the throne.[29]

Things were not always so fraught at Kilcash. 1720 must have been a year of some celebration. For one thing Thomas saw his daughter Honora married to Valentine Browne of Kenmare. The happy occasion was celebrated in two Gaelic poems – *Epithalamium for Lord Kenmare* and *The Good Omen* – written by the distinguished Munster poet Aogán Ó Rathaille (c. 1675-1729), who at the time enjoyed the patronage of the Kenmares:[30]

> Druids and prophets have unravelled
> From the prophecies of Patrick, and Brigid,
> And of holy Colm the truly saintly, sayings
> Which were full of the grace of the Holy Spirit;
> Since a prince of Kilcash has bestowed
> On the King of Killarney his daughter,
> That their sons might inherit the place
> Till the destruction and consummation of the world.[31]

In October of the same year the Duke of Liria, James Fitzjames Stuart (1696-1738) – a son of Thomas's former commander the Duke of

Plate 21:   Archbishop Christopher Butler.

Berwick and his sister-in-law, Honora Burke[32] – arrived in Ireland to stay for five weeks at Kilcash where he 'found all the family in perfect health'.[33] The Duke came on family business – a matter of inheritance – to see Thomas's mother-in-law, the ageing and possibly blind Helen, dowager Countess of Clanrickard, who lived with him and his wife at the castle.³⁴ Here he seems to have considered himself well entertained and of Ireland he wrote:

> In winter, there is a great quantity of woodcock, and I often went out for a couple of hours before dinner to a wood below Kilcash, and I always came back with a dozen, or a dozen-and-a-half birds.³⁵

Sharing all the troubles and the joys of the times since their marriage in 1696³⁶ was Thomas's wife, Margaret Burke, the Lady Iveagh who is celebrated in the haunting song *Cill Chaise*.³⁷ Born in 1673, Margaret was a daughter of William Bourke, 7th Earl of Clanrickard (d. 1687) and his second wife Lady Helen MacCarthy (who was the widow of John Fitzgerald of Dromona, Co. Waterford).³⁸ She was already connected to the Butlers as her maternal grandmother was Lady Elizabeth Butler, sister of the 1st Duke of Ormonde.³⁹ Lady Iveagh's family connections were distinguished on all sides as her father had been Lieutenant and later Chief Governor of Galway in the 1630s and her brother, Lord Galway, died at Aughrim fighting for the Jacobite cause.⁴⁰

Plate 22: Margaret, Viscountess Iveagh and signature.

In 1689 she had married her first husband, Bryan Magennis, Lord Iveagh of Co. Down. Magennis sat in the Parliament of James II, for whom he raised a regiment of cavalry and a regiment of infantry. In 1690 he was governor of Drogheda which he surrendered without resistance to William III's forces. The following year he was attainted as a rebel and he was one of the negotiators of the Articles of Limerick. As a result of this he accepted English recommendations of service to the Austrian Crown, who, though Catholic, were allies of King William. To this end he sailed from Cork to Hamburg in 1692 leading two thousand men.[41] He died fighting for Austria in Hungary in 1696, a fate common to many of the Irish exiles.[42]

Other personal tragedies marred Lady Iveagh's life. It was not just her husbands who predeceased her, as she also saw her eldest son Richard killed in a fall from a horse in 1738[43] and her second son, Walter, die of smallpox while studying at the Royal Academy in Paris in 1711.[44] Her sister Honora, Duchess of Berwick, died having fallen ill after a miscarriage in 1698.[45] Two of her five daughters, Mary and Honora (d. 1730 of smallpox) and their respective husbands, Bryan Kavanagh of Borris (d. 1741) and Valentine Browne (who had by then succeeded to the title 3rd Viscount Kenmare),[46] died before her, as did a third daughter, Margaret (d. 1743) who had married George Mathew of Thurles and Thomastown. (The daughters who survived her were named Helen and Katherine).[47]

The conversion of her remaining son, John, to Protestantism in 1739 must have been a blow to an ageing lady who had so many ties of loyalty to the Catholic faith. Indeed, today – to use the words of her funeral oration – it is still true that Lady Iveagh is 'more renowned for her inimitable piety, sublime virtue, and great Religion; than for her high birth'.[48] The priest who preached at her interment, Richard Hogan,[49] extolled her as one who was more welcoming to priests than almost anyone in Europe[50] and various clerics are said to have owed their education to her benefaction.[51] Fr Hogan also recalled her generosity: 'Her House was open to all Ranks, Degrees, and Stations of People, none excluded....*Killcash* was the known Refuge of poor Gentry of both sexes'.[52]

It is to be hoped that Lady Iveagh's piety does not wholly eclipse other facets of her personality. She was evidently a competent and intelligent woman as well as a religious one. Her husband's will leaves her 'all my corn stock etc. and use of household goods and plate for life' as well as the sum £1000 which figure he had agreed with Lady Iveagh's mother.[53] She was running the Kilcash estate therefore, in the years between the death of her husband and her own death in July 1744 at the age of seventy one.[54]

Consequently Lady Iveagh appears to have been an experienced administrator and it is known that land was transferred to her in March 1740-1.[55] In an undated copy of a letter to one Peter Dally Esq. she addresses the matter of his purchase of the Island of 'Inniserky' (Co. Mayo)[56] which her mother had a lease on. This fact appears to have been kept from Dally when he was in the process of purchasing the island, with the result that Lady Iveagh announced that she would

> prefer a Bill again Cosen ned Burke to know by what right he or his Father held it, for wee recover'd ye possesion of it some years agoe from his Father who had got it after an unfair maner...

She continues:

> I had noe thoughts of beggining any dispute ys time of day but must stand by my mothers act and deed...ye hopes I have yt in honor you won't make use of little advantages again me who have great esteem for you.[57]

By 1742 Lady Iveagh was left as the sole executrix of her husband's will as the other executors had either died or renounced their office.[58] That same year she was a party in a property dispute – concerning land she held in Galway – which came before the House of Lords, the highest court in the land. In July 1743 she writes to one of her nephews, Ullike Bourk (the Burkes seemed to have caused her a lot of trouble). As only one side of the correspondence survives, it is impossible to ascertain the context with full certainty. What is clear is that Lady Iveagh could be charming while at the same time prioritising the interests of her offspring. In the letter she says that she would receive:

> the greatest pleasure and comfort imaginable to have this old business settled in an amicable way and to the advantage of both sides as you say but I am now quite out of the case for ['tis?] my childrens fortunes and the deeds are in my possession wch it can't be thought that I'le ever part with till I see them satisfyed.[59]

The letter ends with her signing off as an affectionate aunt who looked forward to her nephew's next visit.

Popular lore tells of Lady Iveagh attending three masses a day. This may in fact have been so. However, this was a woman who lived the early part of her life in a time of war and who ended her days in the harsh 1740s. During twenty one months in 1740-1, known as *bliadhain an áir* ('the year of the slaughter')[60] a famine and the associated diseases – the culmination of seven seasons of unusual weather – are estimated to have killed between 250,000 to 400,000 people, 'implying a higher death rate and proportionately greater impact than the Great Famine'.[61] The effect of the famine was particularly marked in the Golden Vale.[62] Consequently, if Lady Iveagh wanted to extend her hospitality to all comers she must also have been a woman of formidable organisational and financial talents.

The Church in Kilcash in the Eighteenth Century

Our record of the clergy of Kilcash in the 1700s, the era of Colonel Thomas Butler and Lady Iveagh, is quite a complete one. This reminds us that though Archbishop Christopher Butler could not legally set foot on Irish soil, the Registration Act of 1704 allowed Catholic priests to remain in residence and practice in Ireland provided that they register with the County Sessions and provide security for their 'good behaviour'.[63] It is possible, therefore, that, with the exception of the Cromwellian era, popular notions of furtive eighteenth century clergy presiding at mass rocks are exaggerated.[64]

Rev. James Butler, living in Shanbally is recorded as Parish Priest of Kilcash, Kilsheelan and Templetney in 1704. He was succeeded by the Franciscan James Hogan who delivered the funeral orations for both Lady Iveagh and Archbishop Christopher. Rev. Hogan was transferred to Drumcannon in Tramore (Co. Waterford) and he was replaced by Rev. Richard Phelan, a priest whose vigorous denunciation of the Whiteboys* made him so unpopular that he had to be transferred to Tramore in 1785. Between 1785 and 1811 the Rev. Thomas Anglim was Parish Priest and he was succeeded by Rev. James Hally, who lived in the neighbouring village of Ballypatrick.[65]

By this time the Old Kilcash was no longer the centre of parish worship. Burials continued in the old graveyard but Power records that a thatched chapel in the modern village of Kilcash was replaced by a church erected on the same site in 1810.[66]

Two other sacred artefacts of note owe all or part of their history to the Butlers of Kilcash in the eighteenth century. The first of these is a silver chalice still in regular use in the modern Parish of Kilcash which bears the Latin inscription: 'A.D. 1717 Margaret Burke, Viscountess Iveagh gave me as a gift to the Parish of Kilcash'.[67] The second is a relic

---

*A group of agrarian protesters who objected, amongst other things, to the enclosure of common land and the payment of tithes. They were first appeared in Tipperary in the early 1760s where they were particularly active. They were so called for the white shirts they wore over their clothes.

of the true cross. The relic first makes its certain appearance with Walter Butler of Kilcash who in 1632 is recorded as transferring it to his doctor, Garret Fennell with instructions that it was to be kept in Catholic hands. Its subsequent transmission is a complicated one, and it suffices for us to note that it passed through the possession of Helen Butler, daughter of Thomas and Lady Iveagh, who was married to a Colonel Thomas Butler of Westcourt in Callan.[68] The relic eventually passed into the keeping of the Ursuline Convent in Blackrock, Cork (1801) and part of that relic is today in Holy Cross Abbey.[69]

How Walter of Kilcash came to possess the relic is less clear. The *Annals* of the Ursuline Convent in Blackrock identify it with the original Holy Cross relic which was a gift presented to the King of Limerick, Donald O'Brien in the twelfth century, when he established the monastery at Holy Cross for its veneration. The *Annals* speculate that the Butlers rescued the relic at the suppression of the monasteries and that it was thus that it arrived in Walter's keeping.[70]

This account of its history is elsewhere disputed. Another chronicle of its early transmission claims that it was an old Butler heirloom. According to a family will, in 1487 Sir James Butler left his son, Piers Ruadh (subsequently Earl of Ormond, 1515) a fragment of the true cross from whom it passed to Walter, his great-grandson.[71] Relics of the true cross were notoriously prolific in earlier times. Which – if either – account is the correct one is less important than the fact of the association of such an important object of veneration with the vicinity of Kilcash.

John Butler of Kilcash (d. 1766)

John Butler was the only surviving son of Thomas Butler and Lady Iveagh. In July 1739 'John Butler gent. Kilcash' is certified as having converted to the Church of England. In August, having procured a bishop's certificate to prove his conversion, he was duly 'enrolled'.[72] Where do we look for an explanation of the motivation for his conversion? Is it a reaction to the profound Catholicism of his family or was his motivation based in the more pragmatic considerations of inheritance? There is a consensus that the Church of Ireland at the time was a rather inadequate institution often staffed by poor calibre clergy and absentees. For the most part, the Government wished for converts for practical administrative reasons and not from a genuine proselytising spirit.[73] Some of the landowners who 'converted' were said to have had mass said privately in their houses and they sent their sons to have a Catholic education.[74] Whether John Butler was numbered amongst such new members of the Church of Ireland we do not know. However, a certain religious insincerity can be expected of many of the 4,000 Irish Catholics who converted between 1704 and 1771.[75]

As well as being the ultimate heir to his father's estates at Kilcash, John Butler was in line for the property of his guardian, the childless Charles Butler, the Earl of Arran (1671-1758), on whom devolved the Ormonde estates and title since 1715 and the forfeiture of the same by Arran's brother, the 2nd Duke.[76] When Arran died the estates went to his sister, whom Walpole described as 'a young heiress of ninety-nine'.[77] Unsurprisingly she had not long to enjoy her inheritance and when she died in 1760 John became *de jure* Earl of Ormonde, though he never assumed the title.[78] The little else we know of John confirms that he was a man who was careful – though not mean – with his money, a practicality born perhaps of necessity or inherited from the example of his mother. As we have noted, the 1740s were lean years and in 1747 John was informed that at least £700 must be struck off of what his tenants owed him '& most of it justly, as many deny the charge against them, & some are poor'.[79] What John's response to this was is not recorded. He does not seem to have had much choice in the matter, so no generosity can be inferred on his part. What we do know is that in the early 1750s, like other landlords of his day, he began the unpopular enclosure of common land[80] as well as restricting the amount of tillage his tenants could carry out (so that the fertility of the soil was preserved).[81] In March of 1754 we read of his arranging to borrow money at 4½ per cent, so ready money was not to hand.[82]

Such economic constraints do not seem to have prevented him being solicited for favours by importunate relations and acquaintances however,[83] and though we do not know the outcome of any of these suits, we might infer from them that he must not have been a notorious miser, at least amongst his kindred and friends. In any event, he certainly remembered his family generously in his will, particularly its youngest generation (he left £3000 to his niece Mary who lived with him for a while towards the end of his life).[84] Equally, economic problems did not prevent his living abroad, nor did they wholly curtail his enjoyment of the material comforts of the day. Some idea of daily life in the castle can be gleaned from surviving inventories of silver[85] and kitchen furniture [Plate 23] while the more pleasurable features of life are revealed in a letter of 1753 from one Jack Butler who writes to John Butler from Kilcommon,[86] thanking John for his hospitality and inviting him and some mutual friends to come and stay. There, he wrote, 'you may be diverted with cock shooting and hunting in the morning and whist playing and whoreing in the evening'.[87] An admirable day's entertainment indeed!

For a considerable period of time, John seems to have lived or

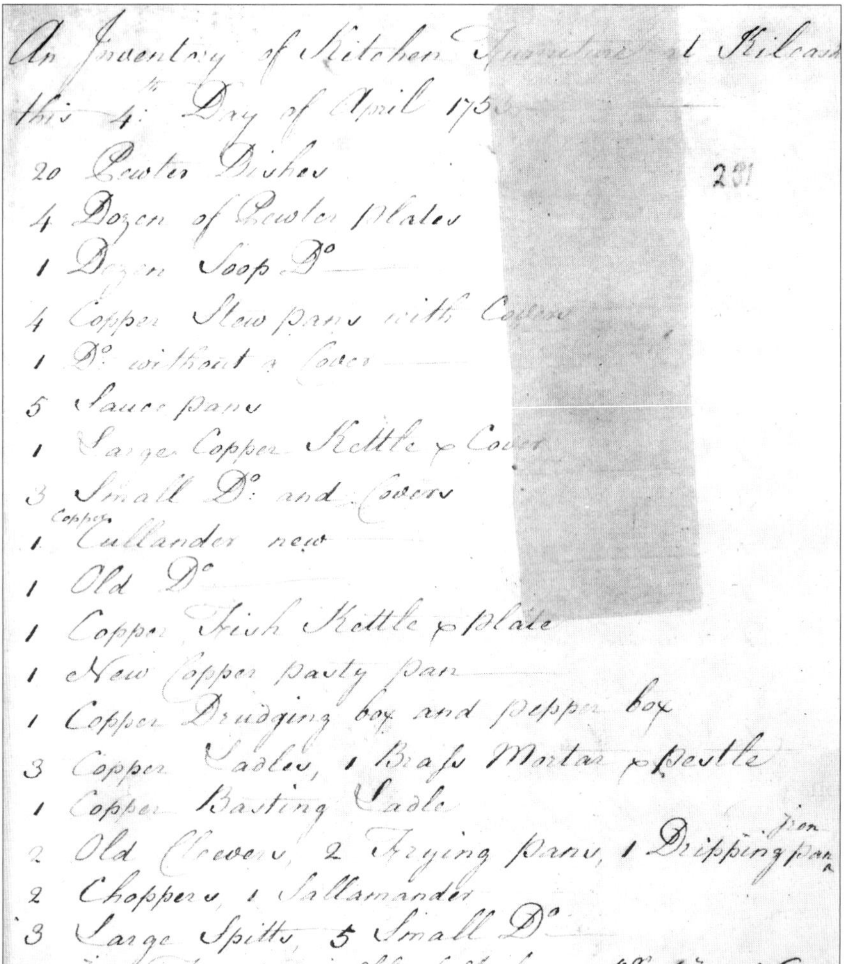

An Inventory of Kitchen Furniture at Kilcash this 4th Day of April 1753

20 Pewter Dishes
4 Dozen of Pewter Plates
1 Dozen Soop Do
4 Copper Stew pans with Covers
1 Do without a Cover
5 Sauce pans
1 Large Copper Kettle & Cover
3 Small Do and Covers
1 Copper Cullander new
1 Old Do
1 Copper Fish Kettle & Plate
1 New Copper pasty pan
1 Copper Dredging box and pepper box
3 Copper Ladles, 1 Brass Mortar & Pestle
1 Copper Basting Ladle
2 Old Cleevers, 2 Frying pans, 1 Iron Dripping pan
2 Choppers, 1 Sallamander
3 Large Spitts, 5 Small Do
4 Iron Trevets, 1 flesh fork, 1 Po of Iron Niggers
1 Large Iron pott Set as a Boiler
3 Small Do
1 Large Brass Skellett, 1 Small Do
2 Grid Irons, 1 pair pott hooks, 1 p:r of hangers
1 Pair of Tongs, a Shovel and Poker
2 Iron Skimmers, 1 Do of Racks, and 1 Jack
2 Doz:n tin petty pans
1 Plate Drainer, two Rolling pins
1 Large Crock, 3 Small Do
1 Tin Cheese Toaster

Plate 23:   Inventory of the kitchen of Kilcash Castle, 1753.

holidayed in England. In 1749 his nephew, Thomas Kavanagh (then in Avignon) writes to him at his lodgings in Bruton Street near Bond Street in London.[88] After this his whereabouts are unclear though there is an extant will of 1752 which has him 'residing in Cork Street in Burlington Gardens in the county of Middlesex' so he is once again (or still) in England.[89] This will provides for the education and upbringing of a daughter, Margaret (doubtless named after Lady Iveagh), who was born that year on the 12th of April and who was then under the care of a nurse. Usually, Butler is said to have died childless[90] and to have married only once – in 1763, at St George's Hanover Square – to Bridget Stacey of Oakingham, Berkshire.[91] The 1752 will attests to the fact that he had a daughter before this (and possibly a wife – she is not mentioned) who may have predeceased him.

Whether or not she was his first wife, Bridget Stacey and John Butler do not seem to have been happy together. Perhaps John's failing health was a strain on the marriage?[92] Whatever the reason, in July 1765 the couple drew up an indenture providing for the fact that 'John Butler and Bridget his wife have agreed to live separate and apart from each other as long as they or either of them shall see fit'. Bridget evidently returned to England as, in addition to £500 which John gave her for her immediate maintenance, he pledged to give her £1000 a year for her upkeep which was to be paid in Sterling.[93] As his life drew to an end, John became very difficult and he had to be cared for in Garryricken by his cousins.[94] In 1766 he died, leaving no descendants as heirs.

1766-1795: The Fall of Kilcash

John Butler was succeeded by his first cousin Walter Butler of Garryricken (1703-1783) who was the son of his father's younger brother John, and Frances, daughter of George Butler of Ballyragget, Co. Kilkenny. Walter never resided at Kilcash as he moved to Kilkenny Castle on his succession to the Ormonde estates. Here he extended generous and splendid hospitality to the local worthies and lived the lifestyle appropriate to the head of one of Ireland's most noble families.[95] Walter had married Eleanor Morres (1711-1793) in 1732.[96] Their fame was eclipsed by that of their youngest daughter, Lady Eleanor Butler, one of the 'Ladies of Llangollen', so called because she lived with her friend Sarah Ponsonby in a ménage which at the time was considered eccentric.[97] When he died, Walter was buried at Kilcash and he was succeeded by his only son, John (1740-1795).

John, known as 'Jack o' the Castle' (the castle being Kilkenny and not Kilcash), was MP for Gowran (1776-83) and later for Kilkenny City (1783-91). He eventually (1791) secured for himself the title of 17th Earl of Ormonde on the grounds that the 2nd Duke had not been attainted

Plate 24: Walter Butler, de jure 16th Earl of Ormonde.

by the Irish parliament.[98] This was an occasion of some civic pride and the bells of Kilkenny rang as canons were fired and lights were lit all over the city.[99]

In his youth John had studied in France returning to Ireland in 1761, an occasion which was celebrated by family rejoicing and Liam Ó Meachair's Gaelic poem *Song for Young John Butler*.[100] A story related by his contemporaries tells how he fell in love with a French lady of rank whom he married to the displeasure of his father. Seemingly, this

Plate 25:   Anne Wandesford.

sorry beauty was abandoned as John sneaked back home with the aid of two Frenchmen whom he later rewarded.[101] Even if the story is untrue or only partially true, it sheds some light on how the local people later remembered him.

John converted to Protestantism in 1764[102] and in 1769 he married 'Anne' Wandesford (1754-1830),[103] the daughter of the John Wandesford (Earl of Castlecomer, Co. Kilkenny). It was an index of his popularity that the newly-wedded couple were greeted by what a contemporary newspaper report called a 'prodigious concourse' of well-wishers and the cathedral bell was rung as bonfires were lit in the streets.[104] The couple lived at Kilkenny with their children Walter (who became 18th Earl), James (who became the 19th Earl after his brother's death in 1820), Charles and Eleanor.

In Kilkenny John enjoyed a moneyed lifestyle with a busy social calendar. In December 1773 a 'coach and chariot' from London are landed for him at Dublin (by this time he is addressed as 'John Butler of Kilcash at the castle, Kilkenny').[105] He was a frequent customer at a tavern called 'The Hole in the Wall' which was run by one of his former valets. This spot soon became the most fashionable haunt in the city while at the same time possessing a reputation for its excessive drinking, its duels and its being a resort of highwaymen.[106] Though even those who were well disposed towards him – thinking him 'well-read and friendly' – admitted that he was 'a hard goer',[107] others were less complimentary. Wolfe Tone said of him that he was 'a drunken beast, without a character of any kind, but that of a blockhead'.[108]

This negative portrait of John does not do him justice though. He appears to have been an ardent politician and was the signatory of a petition for parliamentary reform and the enfranchisement of Catholics.[109] In keeping with the prominence of his position in Kilkenny he contributed to many of the city's celebrations and organisations. Despite a hectic social life he was also a regular attender of the meetings of the board of aldermen. He was generous to the poor and in the freezing winter of 1776 he sent coal to the prisoners in the gaol as well as to forty-two needy townsfolk. Folklore records that he once obtained a pardon for a condemned man only to arrive minutes too late as the body was being taken down from the gallows.[110] His willingness to help others is further demonstrated when in 1787 he personally contributed one hundred guineas towards flood relief to the people of Irishtown (Kilkenny).[111]

Whatever his relative faults and merits, John's demise was the occasion of the last moment of Kilcash's glory. Apparently it was a lavish affair and luncheon was served to all who attended. At the time, the great hall of the house is described as hanging with paintings and the park was well stocked with deer.[112]

Jack o' the Castle is the last of the Butlers to be buried in Kilcash. His son, Walter (1770-1820) became the 18th Earl at the age of 25. Educated at Eton, he was elected MP for Kilkenny (1790-95) and he became a close companion of the Prince Regent. Though tradition records his positive side (in an account of when in 1811 he rushed from London to successfully champion the cause of innocent defendants before a Special Commission),[113] a contemporary remarked

Plate 26:   Walter Butler, 18th Earl of Ormonde.

of his intellectual ability that it was 'blunted by dissipation or absorbed in the licentious influence of a fashionable connection'.[114] Evidently, he lived the life of a gentleman, even fighting a duel against an army captain in 1800 in Ringsend, Dublin (though shots were exchanged, no one was injured).[115] It may have been that it was in order to sustain the improvident lifestyle of fashionable London that he sold the materials of Kilcash 'for a trifling consideration' to a merchant from Carrick-on-Suir called James Power (*c.* 1800).[116] Before this, the family paintings (including a painting of Lady Iveagh and of her sister Honora) and other valuables were removed from Kilcash to Kilkenny,[117] and the long, consecutive process of Kilcash's crumbling began.

The famous trees of Kilcash were sold in two lots in 1797 and in 1801: in 1797 the timber on the avenue that went to the Carrick road 'together with the trees in the Church-grove and Deer-park, consisting of fine oak, ash, beech, and elm' were offered for sale,[118] while in 1801 the remaining timber on the estate was advertised.[119] By the first half of the nineteenth century the 'only vestiges now remaining ... are the walls of the castle'.[120] At around the same time part of the Kilcash estate was sold to a Mr Edward Sheil (d. 1819);[121] the need for liquid money was more pressing than that of holding on to the family's capital assets (at least until 1811 when Walter sold the family's hereditary right to the prisage of wines to the crown for the grand sum of £216,000). In 1891, a little less than a hundred years after its partial dismantling, Kilcash castle was merely a liability taking up valuable acreage and Patrick Ryan, an Ormonde tenant, had his rent reduced by the value of one rood of land for the ground upon which the ruined castle now stands.[122]

> It's the cause of my long affliction
> To see your neat gates knocked down,
> The long walks affording no shade now
> And the avenue overgrown,
> The fine house that kept out the weather,
> Its people depressed and tamed;
> And their names with the faithful departed,
> The Bishop and Lady Iveagh![123]

References
1. William Carrigan (1905), 318.
2. There is some dispute about the relative ages of these two brothers. Renehan records Christopher as being the eldest in the family, claiming that he was passed over in the succession because of his vocation. [Laurence F. Renehan, 303.] On the other hand, we are sure that the third brother, Lieutenant Colonel John Butler, was younger than Thomas as apart from the question of succession, the fact is explicitly mentioned in uncatalogued indentures in NLI Packing Case 12988 (5).
3. Skehan Papers vol. 5. James III was the last of the Stuarts accorded this privilege by the popes.
4. K. Danaher & J. G. Simms eds. (1962), 98.
5. John J. Silke (1976), 609-10.

6. James, the 2nd Duke of Ormond (1665-1745) fought for William during the war and even entertained him in Kilkenny Castle. In the 1700s though, due to his alienation from the Whig-dominated political establishment in England, he ended up embracing the Jacobite cause.
7. J. T. Gilbert ed. (1971), 206-7.
8. Lillian Tate ed. (1959), 189.
9. Sheila Mulloy (1983-4), III, 72.
10. The names of the officers who served under him can be found in John D'Alton (1860), II, 402.
11. Ibid., III, 49; 90 q.v.
12. K. Danaher & J. G. Simms eds. (1962), 99.
13. Ibid.
14. In his letter to Thomas from Clonmel Würtemberg does not mention that he is protecting Richard, though he does mention his respect for Thomas's family. Evidently Thomas found out about Richard's being 'at this moment under your protection' [K. Danaher and J. G. Simms eds. (1962), 99] from some other source. Whether there was an implicit threat in Würtemberg's 'protection' of the ageing Richard we cannot know. Regardless, this must have been a question which Thomas asked himself and it must have been an additional pressure on him.
15. Patrick C. Power (1989), 84. See also J. T. Gilbert ed. (1971), 148. K. Danaher & J. G. Simms eds. (1962), 123.
16. See J. G. Simms (1969), 227.
17. Sheila Mulloy (1983-4), II, 388.
18. Patrick C. Power (1989), 84.
19. See William Burke (1983/1907), 142-3.
20. Patrick Fagan ed. (1995), II, 64.
21. 'penal laws' in S. J. Connolly (1998), 438. See also L. J. Proudfoot (1993), 197.
22. William Wilde notes the scarcity and dearness of corn in 1728-9. [E. Mary Crawford ed. (1989), 11].
23. Letter dated 27/10/1729. NLI Ormond Papers MS. 2478/37.
24. NLI Ormonde Papers MS. 2478/17. His daughter married in 1720, so it is obviously after this date.
25. Thomas Morris (1955), 2.
26. 9 William III, cap. 26.
27. Thomas Morris (1955), 4.
28. Skehan [Skehan Papers, vol. 5] mentions Ryan, Edward Tyrrell and McGrath in this role.
29. Thomas P. Power (1993), 239. For the material in this paragraph see also Maureen Wall (1989), 40-1.
30. Aogán Ó Rathaille (1911), 172-175; 232-235. To be precise, *The Good Omen* was written to celebrate the betrothal while the *Epithalamium* celebrated the marriage.
31. Aogán Ó Rathaille (1911), 233.
32. Honora Burke had been married to the celebrated Jacobite commander Patrick Sarsfield (1655-1693). After his death the Duke of Berwick fell in love with her and they were married (against King James's wishes) in the royal chapel at St Germain-en-Laye (a Jacobite centre south of Paris) in 1695. Honora's charm and grace was a matter of some comment by her contemporaries. [See Charles Petrie (1953), 101-2].
33. Charles Petrie ed. (1951), 98.
34. Charles Petrie [(1975), 153] is incorrect in suggesting that the dowager Countess

was called Lettice. Lettice Shirley was the first wife of the William Bourke, Earl of Clanrickard (d. 1687) and she died in 1655. Helen, a widow when she became the Earl's second wife, survived him and remarried. Her third husband, Thomas Bourke died between 1718-20 after which she appears to have gone to live in Kilcash. Helen's will is dated 6th August 1720 and it was proved on June 27th 1722. [See H. A. Doubleday and Lord Howard de Walden eds. (1911-40), III, 232-3].

35. Charles Petrie (1975), 154.
36. The date is recorded in a rather tortuous, but informative passage in Thomas Burke (1762), 268: *'Thomam Butlerum*, Chiliarcham, seu *Colonellum*, ut vocant, Peditum sub Rege *Jacobo* II, de Anno 1696 *Margaritae de Burgo, Gulielmi*, Septimi *Clanrickardiae* Comitis, & *Hiberniae* Proregis, seu Justitarij, Filiae, & Briani Magennis, Domini Vicecomitis de *Iveagh*, in Agro *Dunensi*, Viduae, Matriomonio conjunctum'.
37. An anonymous note appended to the copy of Lodge's *Peerage* in the library of the Irish Folklore Department in University College Dublin (UCDF) records that the wedding took place in St Germain-en-Laye. Though we are aware of no other reference to the marriage it seems unlikely that this in fact was the case as the marriage is not recorded in the published Jacobite records from the parish [C. E. Lart (1910)]. In the light of the fact that Lady Iveagh's sister Honora was later married here, there is the possibility that the note's author confused the two sisters.
38. H. A. Doubleday and Lord Howard de Walden eds. (1911-40), III, 232-3. For Lady Helen's subsequent marriage see the note on Liria's visit to Kilcash in 1720 above.
39. A fact highlighted in her funeral sermon. [Richard Hogan (1744), 12].
40. Katherine M. Lanigan (1985), 398.
41. J. G. Simms (1986), 630.
42. For Magennis's life see H. A. Doubleday and Lord Howard de Walden eds. (1911-40), VIII, 351-2. A briefer account of his career appears in John O'Daly ed. (1850), 201.
43. In a letter of 6/10/1864 John Dunne records that two elderly brothers of his acquaintance - Joe and William Lawrence, aged 76 and 80 respectively - recall a story of their father's (he was a retainer of Walter Butler of Garryricken d. 1783) recounting how Richard was on his way to convert to the Church of Ireland when he fell from his horse, fatally striking his head against a stone. [UCDF, Prim Manuscripts]. It seems possible that this 'Catholic' moral is a conflation of the fate of Richard with the conversion of John as both these events took place within a year of one another.
44. Skehan Papers vol. 42. J. F. McCarthy (1954), 31 names Walter as the eldest son.
45. Charles Petrie (1953), 109. She showed some signs of having consumption.
46. Katherine M. Lanigan (1985), 398.
47. Helen first married a Mr Esmond who accidentally shot himself when out fowling in 1736 and then subsequently married Colonel Richard Butler of Westcourt, Callan. Katherine was the third wife of James Mandeville of Ballydine, Co. Tipperary.
48. Richard Hogan (1744), 5.
49. Hogan would later preach at the funeral of Archbishop Christopher Butler who was buried at Kilcash in 1754 [See Richard Hogan (1754)].
50. Ibid., 18-19.
51. Including Fr John Lane, once a candidate for *Caoineadh Cill Chais* and less well

known figures such as Fr John Shea (d. 1794), PP of Kilrossenty and Fews [Patrick Power (1937), 159].
52. Richard Hogan (1754), 18. It is difficult to disentangle eulogy from history in Hogan's sermon. Certainly the tradition of Lady Iveagh's piety and generosity survive in Kilcash to this day and the unusual reference to 'poor Gentry of both sexes' has a ring of authenticity about it.
53. Will of Thomas Butler (1730). NLI Ormond Papers, Special List 38, (c) 431a.
54. A fact attested to by various uncatalogued indentures in NLI Packing Case 12988. 5 Some idea of the size of the estate and the nature of its holdings outside the immediate vicinity of Kilcash can be garnered from leases in NLI Packing Case 12673.1. (Note that the NLI has two packing cases with this code number).
55. NLI Ormond Papers 2478/113.
56. The *Census of Ireland* [(1861), 537] identifies an Inisherkin island off the coast of Mayo. The island, a little over 30 acres in size, is in the parish of Burrishoole.
57. NLI Ormond Papers 2482/429.
58. Wallace Clare ed. (1932), 78.
59. NLI Ormonde Papers MS. 2478/251.
60. J. L. McCracken (1986), 34.
61. David Dickson (1989), 97. It seems that Munster was particularly badly affected. [ibid., 98]. A contemporary account speaks of carriages being able to drive over the frozen Shannon in the winter of 1739. Due to the harsh conditions Archbishop Christopher Butler relaxed the obligation for the Lenten fast. [Skehan Papers, vol. 6]. We note however that our records of the gravestone inscriptions in the old Kilcash cemetery do not show an unusual death rate in this period [Appendix 1].
62. David Dickson (1997), 69.
63. L. J. Proudfoot (1993), 196. 1089 priests registered under the terms of the Act.
64. Recent research suggests that mass rocks were more the result of a lack of resources on the part of an area rather than an indication of official persecution. [S. J. Connolly ed. (1998), 352]. Local tradition identifies a mass rock nearby in the neighbouring townland of Ballypatrick.
65. For the information in this paragraph see Patrick Power (1912), 148.
66. Ibid., 147.
67. The chalice stands 22cm tall. The bowl, which is plated on the inside in gold, is 8.5 cm in diameter.
68. See James Maher (1954), 34-5 and S. P. Little (1982), 193.
69. The sisters made a gift of a portion of the relic to Holy Cross in 1977. The abbey retained the silver reliquary with the Ormond coat of arms in which it had been kept. [Letter from Sister Ursula Clarke, Ursuline Convent, Blackrock to Mrs Una Power of Clonmel, September 4th 1995]. We are grateful to Mrs Una Power for sharing her information on the relic and its history with us.
70. We are grateful to Una Power for the transcript of the *Annals*. We note that Walter is recorded as posting watchmen at Holy Cross in 1601 [Historical Manuscripts Commission (1895-1912), I, 3].
71. S. P. Little (1982), 193.
72. Eileen O'Byrne ed. (1981), 34.
73. See Thomas P. Power (1990), 101.
74. J. L. McCracken (1986), 38.
75. The figures [in L. J. Proudfoot (1993), 195] represent formal, registered conversions.
76. In his will Thomas Butler left the lease of the deer-park in Carrick to his son and

he appointed Arran as his guardian. After Lady Iveagh's death, the Kilcash estate was to pass to him. [Will of Thomas Butler (1730). NLI Ormond Papers, Special List 38, (c) 431a].

77. Quoted in H. A. Doubleday and Lord Howard de Walden eds. (1911-40), X, 162, n.
78. Thomas P. Power (1993), 112.
79. NLI Kavanagh Papers.
80. Thomas P. Power (1993), 166-7.
81. Ibid., 171.
82. NLI Ormond Papers 2479/121.
83. See *inter alia* NLI Ormond Papers 2479/272 and 2479/391.
84. Will of John Butler (1764). NLI Ormond Papers, Special List 38, (c) 471a.
85. Inventory of items being transferred to Dublin, November 1747. NLI Ormond Papers MS. 2621/229.
86. There are two Kilcommons in Tipperary N.R., one near Thurles and another near Borrisokane. Near Clogheen in Tipperary S.R. there is a Kilcommon Beg and a Kilcommon More. [*Census of Ireland* (1861), 555).
87. NLI Ormond Papers 2479/175.
88. NLI Kavanagh Papers.
89. NLI MS. D27,097. This will has a signature which matches that on his letters. See, *inter alia* NLI Ormond Papers 2479/329. From Registry MS., book 180, no. 121720 we know that Butler is in England in July 1756 (probably Middlesex if the witnesses' addresses are anything to go by). However, a letter of 1753 sent to him by a niece is addressed to Kilcash [NLI Ormond Papers 2479/167] as is the abovementioned letter of Jack Butler of Kilcommon (1753).
90. Thus Lord Dunboyne (1991), 20.
91. See Katherine M. Lanigan (1985), 394; *Burke's Peerage* (1980), 2044 and H. A. Doubleday and Lord Howard de Walden eds. (1911-40), X, 163. After John's death, Bridget married a Rev. Alleyne Waller of Surrey (1771). We note that not only was Bridget English, but she later married an Englishman. Though inconclusive, this suggests a circle which was based in England and not Tipperary.
92. An illness is mentioned in his own letters of 1757 [Ormond papers 2479/329] and 1758 [NLI Kavanagh Papers, no. 13].
93. NLI Ormond Papers, Special List 38, (c) 472.
94. John's insanity is recorded in a letter of John Dunne's dated 6/10/1864. Here, Dunne - on the strength of the memories of the Lawrence brothers (see above, the death of John's brothers) - asserts that due to his illness John was very difficult before he died and that he ended his days in the care of the Butlers of Garryricken. John's insanity is mentioned in Thomas P. Power (1993), 112 q.v.
95. W. G. Neely (1989), 211.
96. Her death was commemorated in the anonymous Gaelic lament *Caoineadh Don Bhantiarna Bhuiltéar*. [Reproduced in Dáithí Ó hÓgáin ed. (1980), 50-1].
97. The couple were known for wearing masculine clothing. That the relationship - which lasted fifty years - might have been a lesbian one can only be conjectured.
98. C. A. Empey 'Ormond (Butler)' in S. J. Connolly (1998), 417.
99. W. G. Neely (1989), 165.
100. *Amhrán do Sheán Óg Builtéar*. For the text see Dáithí Ó hÓgáin ed. (1980), 49.
101. Ibid., 105.
102. Folklore records that John conformed to the Church of Ireland publicly while remaining a Catholic and attending mass privately. [John Dunne in UCDF, Prim Manuscripts].

103. Her real name was Susan Frances Elizabeth but she was known as 'Anne'.
104. W. G. Neely (1989), 213.
105. NLI Ormond Papers 2480/185.
106. W. G. Neely (1989), 213-4.
107. Barrington quoted in H. A. Doubleday and Lord Howard de Walden eds. (1911-40), X, 164, n.
108. Recorded in his diary for March 14th 1796. See William Theobald Wolfe Tone ed., II, 50.
109. W. G. Neely (1989), 164.
110. John Dunne writing in UCDF, Prim Manuscripts (c. 1865). We are grateful to Dáithí Ó hÓgáin for drawing our attention to this.
111. W. G. Neely (1989), 213.
112. Katherine M. Lanigan (1985), 397.
113. John Dunne writing in UCDF, Prim Manuscripts (c. 1865). We are grateful to Dáithí Ó hÓgáin for drawing our attention to this.
114. Quoted in H. A. Doubleday and Lord Howard de Walden eds. (1911-40), X, 162, n.
115. James Kelly (1995), 208.
116. P. Lynch (1815), xxvii n. Power was a very common name in Carrick at the time. See British Museum MS, 11,722 (A census of Carrick-on-Suir in 1799) a copy of which is in on microfilm in the National Library of Ireland.
117. Katherine M. Lanigan (1985), 397. The portrait of Honora is still on display in Kilkenny castle while that of Lady Iveagh is in the possession of the Van den Steen de Jehay family (Belgium) who are trustees of the Ormonde estates.
118. *Saunder's Newsletter, and Daily Advertiser,* No. 12455, Monday April 24th, 1797. A similar advertisement appeared in *Finn's Leinster Journal,* 31:30, April 12th-15th, 1797.
119. *Finn's Leinster Journal,* 35:3, January 7th-10th, 1801. The advertisement was rerun throughout January and February. We are grateful to Mr Joe Norton (Dúchas) for bringing these to our attention.
120. John O'Daly (1850), 196n.
121. See NLI MS. 1107. The sale later proved unsatisfactory. It seems that Mr Sheil undertook to pay a substantial debt left outstanding by John Butler to the Dublin Infirmary. However, the debt was still outstanding in the 1830s when it became the subject of a lawsuit between the Earl of Ormonde and the Infirmary.
122. NLI MS. 23,965. Rent book for Kilcash.
123. This is the second stanza of Kilcash from the translation by Eiléan Ní Chuilleanáin which can be found in full in Chapter IV.

Chapter IV

The Literary Heritage

Cill Chaise
Today Kilcash is probably best remembered, neither for its history nor for the antiquity of its monuments but for the popular Irish song *Cill Chaise* (*Kilcash*) which mourns the passing of the era of Lady Iveagh.

Once a staple of the schools' Irish syllabus, the song was attributed to Father John Lane a Parish Priest of Carrick-on-Suir who died in 1776.[1] However, this attribution is certainly mistaken. Fr Lane died long before Kilcash was ruined and the sale of its timber did not begin until 1797. More recently, it has been suggested that the song was composed by the poet Pádraig Ó Néill.[2] However, though there are interesting arguments for this, it is hardly certain.

By its very nature, *Cill Chaise* was intended to be sung. Its air appears to be that of *Bliain sa taca so a phós mé* (*This time twelve months I married*), an old Munster air which was collected by George Petrie in Clare and published in 1855.[3] (Other references to the song's air are noted in Appendix 3).[4]

Cill Chaise was probably composed in the early nineteenth century after the sale of the remaining timber from the Kilcash estate and the ruin of the castle. The earliest reference we have found to a written copy of the song is a passing one in a letter written by John Dunne in February 1843. In this letter Dunne notes that he wrote down the song from the singing of one Eil[een] Hickey of Poulacapple (near Mullinahone, Tipperary S. R.). After this Dunne's transcription of the song appeared – seemingly without his permission – in printed form somewhere in the U. S., though whether in Irish or in English translation, we cannot say.[5]

The earliest extant manuscript copies of the text date from the mid-nineteenth century, so forty years or so elapsed between the song's original composition and its being recorded in any of its extant versions. Though modern Irish editions have been published in the recent past[6] it was felt that the textual history of the song was involved enough to require a scholarly version which lists the variant readings of the available sources. To this end Professor Dáithí Ó hÓgáin has prepared an Irish text with a literal English prose translation. The sources used by Professor Ó hÓgáin, along with the variant readings to be found in them and a note on the vocabulary employed in the poem, are to be found in Appendix 3. His Irish text of *Cill Chaise* follows:

CILL CHAISE

  Créad a dhéanfaimid feasta gan adhmad,
  tá deireadh na gcoillte ar lár;
  níl trácht ar Chill Chais ná a teaghlach,
4 is ní bainfear a cling go bráth;
  an áit úd ina gcónaíodh an deighbhean
  a fuair gradam is meidhir tar mhná,
  bhíodh iarlaí ag tarraing tar toinn ann,
8 is an tAifreann binn á rá.

  Is é mo chreach fhada is mo léan goirt
  do gheataí breá néata ar lár,
  an *avenue* ghreanta faoi shaothar
12 is gan foscadh ar aon taobh den *walk*,
  an chúirt bhreá a sileadh an braon di
  is an ghasra shéimh go tláith,
  is in leabhar na marbh do léitear
16 an tEaspag is *Lady Iveagh*!

  Ní chluinim fuaim lacha ná gé ann
  ná fiolair ag déanadh aeir cois cuain,
  ná fiú na mbeacha chum saothair
20 a thabharfadh mil agus céir don tslua,
  níl ceol binn milis na n-éan ann
  le hamharc an lae a dhul uainn,
  ná an chuaichín i mbarra na ngéag ann,
24 - ó, 'sí a chuirfeadh an saol chum suain!

  Nuair a thigeann na poic faoi na sléibhte
  is an gunna lena dtaobh is an líon
  féachann siad anuas le léan ar
28 an mbaile a fuair *sway* in gach tír;
  an fhaiche bhreá aoibhinn ina réabacha
  is gan foscadh ar aon taobh ón tsín,
  páirc an *phaddock* ina *dairy*
32 mar a mbíodh an eilit ag déanadh a scíth'!

	Tá ceo ag titim ar chraobhaibh ann
	ná glanann le grian ná lá,
	tá smúit ag titim ón spéir ann,
36	is a cuid uisce go léir ag trá;
	níl coll, níl cuileann, níl caora ann,
	ach clocha agus maolchlocháin;
	páirc na foraoise gan chraobh ann,
40	is d'imigh an *game* chum fáin!

	Anois mar bharr ar gach mí-ghreann
	chuaigh prionsa na nGael tar sáil,
	anonn le hainnir na míne
44	fuair gairm sa bhFrainc is sa Spáinn -
	anois tá a cuallacht á caoineadh,
	gheibheadh airgead buí agus bán,
	'sí ná tógfadh seilbh na ndaoine,
48	acht caraid na bhfíorbhochtán.

	Aitím ar Mhuire is ar Íosa
	go dtaga sí arís chughainn slán,
	go mbeidh rincí fada ag gabháil timpeall,
52	ceol veidhlín is tinte cnámh,
	go dtógfar an baile seo ár sinsear
	Cill Chais bhreá arís go hard,
	is go brách nó go dtiocfaidh an díleann
56	ní fheicfear í arís ar lár!

Prose Translation of Cill Chaise

1   *What shall we do henceforth without timber – the last of the woods is laid low. There is no mention of Kilcash or its household, and its bell shall never be tinkled again. In the place where the generous woman used to live – she who gained esteem and affection above all women – earls used to visit there from overseas, and the melodious Mass used to be read.*

9   *It is my long-lasting loss and my bitter sorrow that your fine neat gates are laid low, the well-designed avenue is overgrown and there is no shelter on any side of the walk, the fine mansion from which rain used to run off and the gentle company is dejected, and in the book of the dead are read the [names of the] Bishop and Lady Iveagh.*

17 *I do not hear the noise of a duck or of a goose there, or eagles*

soaring into the air by the refuge, or even the bees undertaking work who would give honey and wax to the people. The melodious sweet music of the birds is not there as the light of day goes away from us, nor is the little cuckoo on the tops of the branches there – oh, she it is who would put everybody to sleep!

25 *When the gallants come through the mountains, with the gun and the hunting-net alongside them, they look down with sadness on the townland which won fame in every territory. The fine pleasant lawn is torn up, with shelter on no side from the weather! The paddock-field is turned into a dairy, where the doe used to take its rest!*

33 *Fog is falling on the branches there, which does not clear in the sun or daylight, mist is falling from the sky there, and all its water is ebbing away. There is no hazel, no holly, no berries there, but rocks and bare stony ground. The forest-park has no branches there, and the game has all gone away.*

41 *Now, to top every misfortune, the prince of the Gaels went over the sea, from here with the gentle maiden he was called away to France and to Spain. Now her company are lamenting her – they who used to receive gold and silver. She it was who would not take away the people's possessions, but who was the friend of the very poorest.*

49 *I beseech Mary and Jesus that she may come safely to us again, that long dances may be going on all around, violin-music and bonfires; that this place of our ancestors may be built up once more as fine Kilcash, and forever until the deluge comes it will not be seen to be laid low again!*

The rendering of *Cill Chaise* into English has been the task of a number of distinguished Irish poets, the best known of whom are Michael Cavanagh, Thomas Kinsella, and Frank O'Connor.[7] Having established an Irish text it seemed appropriate to look for a poetic translation based on this, rather than any other version. To this end the poet Eiléan Ní Chuilleanáin has provided this English translation for us.

KILCASH
What will we do now for timber
With the last of the woods laid low –
No word of Kilcash nor its household,
Their bell is silenced now,
Where the lady lived with such honour,
No woman so heaped with praise,
Earls came across oceans to see her
And heard the sweet words of Mass.

It's the cause of my long affliction
To see your neat gates knocked down,
The long walks affording no shade now
And the avenue overgrown,
The fine house that kept out the weather,
Its people depressed and tamed;
And their names with the faithful departed,
The Bishop and Lady Iveagh!

The geese and the ducks' commotion,
The eagle's shout are no more,
The roar of the bees gone silent,
Their wax and their honey store
Deserted. Now at evening
The musical birds are stilled
And the cuckoo is dumb in the treetops
That sang lullaby to the world.

Even the deer and the hunters
That follow the mountain way
Look down upon us with pity,
The house that was famed in its day;
The smooth wide lawn is all broken,
No shelter from wind and rain;
The paddock has turned to a dairy
Where the fine creatures grazed.

Mist hangs low on the branches
No sunlight can sweep aside,
Darkness falls among daylight
And the streams are all run dry;
No hazel, no holly or berry,
Bare naked rocks and cold;
The forest park is leafless
and all the game gone wild.

And now the worst of our troubles,
She has followed the prince of the Gaels –
He has borne off the gentle maiden,
Summoned to France and to Spain
Her company laments her
That she fed with silver and gold:
One who never preyed on the people
But was the poor souls' friend

My prayer to Mary and Jesus
She may come safe home to us here
To dancing and rejoicing
To fiddling and bonfire
That our ancestors' house will rise up,
Kilcash built up anew
And from now to the end of the story
May it never again be laid low.

Cill Chaise is written from the perspective of specific historical events, yet its subject matter was so general that it spoke to the wider experience of Irish society and thus passed into popular lore. An index of its popularity is the number of compositions which parody its opening line, giving us the now forgotten twentieth century ditties *Cad a dhéanfaimid feasta gan Gaeilge* ('What will we do henceforth without the Irish language?') and *Cad dhéanfaimid feasta gan grievance* ('What will we do henceforth without grievance).[8]

In consequence of this popularity, the woods of Kilcash have attained a symbolic significance and the poem's opening 'What shall we do henceforth without timber?' spoke to local situations well beyond the confines of Tipperary. Indeed, the opening image of the poem is not a unique one. Aogán Ó Rathaille mourned the loss of the great estate of the Brownes of Kerry with the line 'Is díth creach bhur gcoillte ar feóchadh' ('Woe, your woods withering away'). The downfall of families dear to the Gaelic Irish went hand in hand with the felling of trees.[9] (As Ó Rathaille had a connection with Kilcash through his celebration of the marriage of Valentine Browne and Honora Butler, perhaps the distinguished poet's precedent is being invoked in the lament for Kilcash?)

Cill Chaise is no dream allegory, yet it has some – admittedly limited – similarities with the form of Irish poetry known as the *aisling*. This genre, associated with Ó Rathaille, commonly involves the dreaming and downtrodden poets being led by a beautiful lady to a vision of political redemption in the form of veiled references to the house of Stuart, the Catholic pretenders to the English throne. *Cill Chaise* has an aisling's politically subjugated air and it too looks to a revolution which will restore the old (Gaelic) order. It also looks for salvation in the figure of a lovely woman.

The beauty of lost Kilcash is strikingly evoked in the song. There is a rich composition of place recalling not only its trees but its walks, lawn, great gates and game parks. The song dwells particularly on the aural qualities of the now lost calls of the geese and the ducks, the

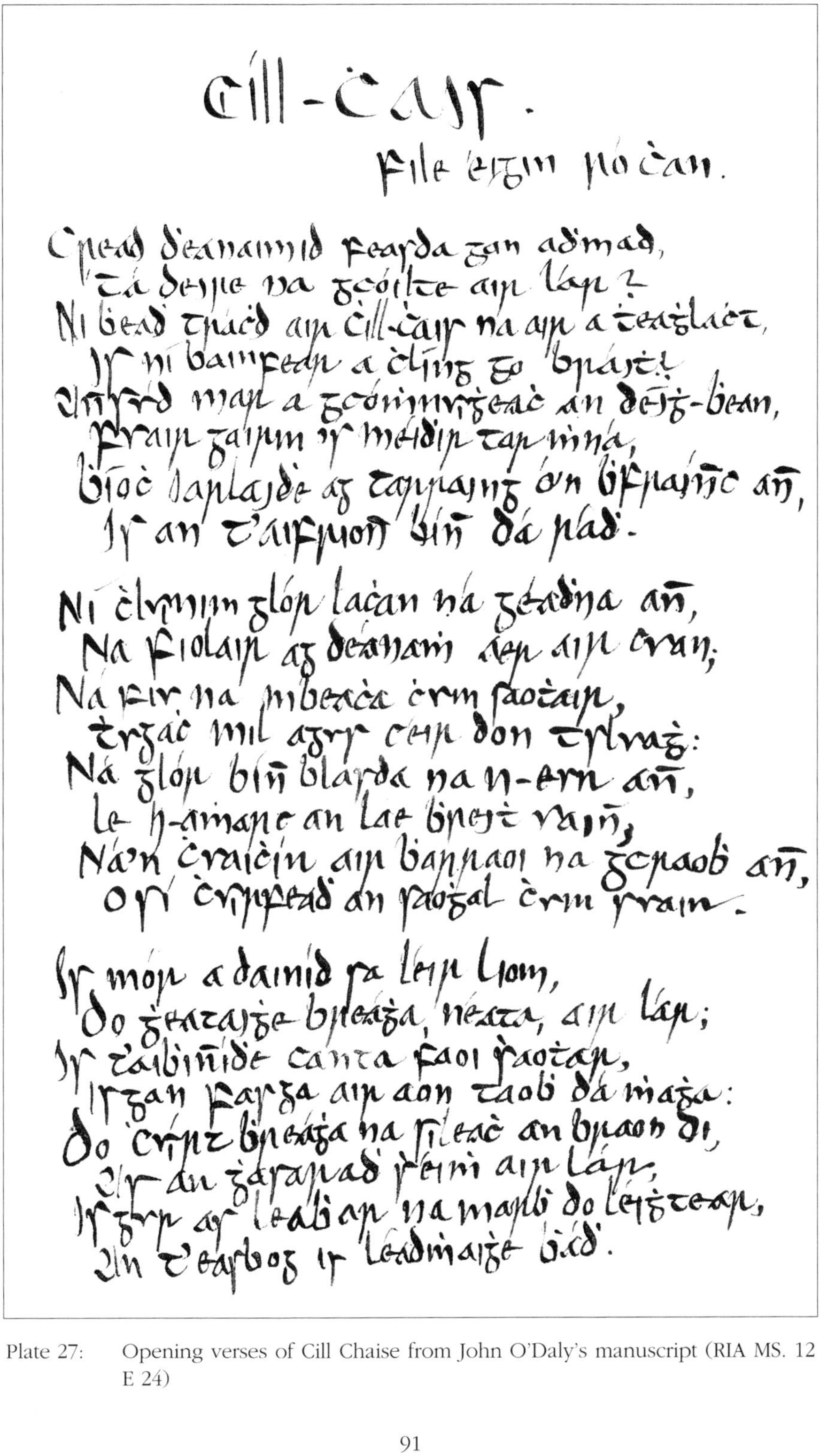

Cill-Cais.

File eigin gan ainm.

Créad déanaimid feasda gan adhmad,
Tá deire na gcoillte air lár?
Ní bead trácd air Cill-cais na air a teaghlach,
Is ní baintear a cling go bráth,
An áit úd ina gcómhnuigheach an deigh-bean,
Fuair gairm is meidir tar mná,
Bhíoch iarlaidhe ag tarraing ón bhFrainc ann,
Is an t-aifreann bínn dá rádh.

Ní chluinim glór lachan na géadhna ann,
Na fiolair ag déanam aer air crann;
Na fir, na mbeacha chum saothair,
Trághach mil agus céir don tsluagh;
Ná glór binn blasda na n-éan ann,
Le h-amarc an lae breith uain,
Na'n chuaichín air bharraoi na gcraobh ann,
Ó's ní cuirfeadh an saoghal chum fuain.

Is mór a dhainid fa leith liom,
Do geataigthe breagha, nochta, air lár;
Is taibhnide canta faoi faothar,
Is gan fasga air aon taobh dá mbáth:
Do cruit breagha na bfileach an bruaon di,
Is an garradh féin air lár,
Is iúr ag leabhair na marbh do leigtear,
An t-earbog is leabhmhaighe biadh.

Plate 27: Opening verses of Cill Chaise from John O'Daly's manuscript (RIA MS. 12 E 24)

tinkling bell and the buzzing of the bees. It culminates in an appropriately Catholic invocation of Jesus and Mary, a prayer for the return of former joy and glory which are to endure until the end of things in the second great flood.[10]

For all its specificity of reference, and despite the fact that Lady Iveagh is named directly and that we know that Christopher Butler is the bishop referred to (line 16), the song remains elusive at some points. The earls mentioned in line seven may be Castlehaven and/or Liria,[11] however, the identities of the 'prince of the Gaels' (line 42) and his lady are difficult – if not impossible – to pin down with any certainty.

This is a crux in the interpretation of the poem. The first stanza alludes to and the second stanza names Lady Iveagh (d. 1744) who had died well over half a century before the ruin of Kilcash and the composition of the song. The sixth stanza introduces the prince of the Gaels who left for the Continent with his 'gentle maiden' (line 43). After this point Lady Iveagh appears to be forgotten and the remainder of the poem is a lament for the departed maiden and the gladness and generosity associated with her.

The history of Kilcash after the death of Lady Iveagh provides us with no likely candidates for the prince and his lady. None of the subsequent owners of Kilcash went into exile and for the most part they preferred to live in Kilkenny Castle. It has, however, been suggested that the stanzas refer to Walter, the 18th Earl and his wife and that the song speaks of the Earl's quitting Ireland for England after the Act of Union.[12] Nonetheless, we consider that this is unlikely. After all, the Earl went to England and not to the Catholic Continent and it would be unlikely that a poet lamenting Kilcash would commemorate an absentee couple who sold its timber and left its castle fall into ruin.

Who then might the prince and his lady be? There are a number of possible answers, none of them wholly satisfactory.

Firstly, we note that Jacobite literature proved enduring in Ireland. Long after the defeat of Bonnie Prince Charlie (Charles Edward Stuart, 1720-88) at the Battle of Culloden (Inverness, April 1746) and the effective end of any possibility of a Stuart restoration, Jacobite sympathies remained strong in the popular imagination. Aislings were written as late as 1840[13] and *The Times* described the Jacobite songs as being more dangerous to English rule than O'Connell's Parliament.[14] A local example of this can be found in the eighteenth century poem *Gabha Dubh Chill Chaise* (*The Blacksmith of Kilcash*) in its forty-second line (which coincidentally echoes the same line in *Cill Chaise*): 'Nó Carolus chughainn thar sáile'.[15]

It is unlikely though that *Cill Chaise* speaks of Bonnie Prince Charlie.

As he married at the age of fifty-two his bride never set foot in Ireland. Moreover, shortly after their marriage the twenty year old girl tired of the prince, whom she fled for the security of a Roman convent. Later she lived openly in Paris with her lover.[16] Needless to say the Prince's marriage was not considered a fit subject for Jacobite commemoration.

Alternatively, the 'Prince of the Irish' might recall the Second Duke of Ormonde, James Butler (1665-1745) who lived the latter part of his life in Spain plotting for the Jacobites before ending his days in Avignon. The Duke would have been remembered long after his death as his property and title ultimately passed to John Butler of Kilcash (Lady Iveagh and Thomas Butler's son) and his heirs. James's second marriage in 1685 was to Mary, daughter of the first Baron Capall of Hadham. Thomas Carte (the first Duke's biographer) speaks of Mary's extraordinary merit and John Dryden dedicated *Palamon and Arcite* to her, so she certainly attracted some notice from those around her.[17]

There is a problem, however, even with this reading. The line introducing the prince begins 'Anois' ('Now'). This conveys a sense of immediacy, suggesting that the poem was written directly after his departure.[18] This obviously will not fit with a date of composition in the early nineteenth century. The puzzle therefore, remains.

One solution that we have considered is that the text which we have today is either lacking some of its original matter or is a composite of more than one song. Oral transmission is a living process and songs were adapted in repetition (in which case the search after the song's 'author' is a difficult task). The description of the prince's maiden as generous and just combined with the restoration of Kilcash's glory in the final stanza would fit very well with the folk memory of Lady Iveagh (indeed, in the nineteenth century, the song was sometimes known as the 'Song for Lady Iveagh'[19]). If lines 41-44 were from another composition (perhaps an earlier Jacobite one), or if some lines were missing, the problem with the poem's narrative would be explained. This possibility highlights the importance of establishing a scholarly text of the song.

The editor of our text of the poem, Professor Ó hÓgáin, has tentatively suggested a possible alternative. In a note he prepared for us with his edition of the poem he writes:

"The use of the form *caraid* (line 48) is of interest. In the singular, meaning 'a friend', it would be a literary usage. In dialectal Irish, however, it would be understood rather as a variant plural of *cairde* ('friends'), and this might be significant with regard to the apparently confused narrative of the song.

"Alteration in oral transmission could have projected the image of Lady Iveagh from lines 5-8, 15-16 onto the two final stanzas – perhaps assisted by the grammatical reference to Cill Chais as *í* ('she') in line 56. Accordingly, the original version of these lines may have referred to 'the prince*s* of the Gaels' having been called during the 18th century to the Continent to serve the Catholic cause (that of the Virgin Mary, 'the gentle maiden'). The reference to Lady Iveagh in line 6 already paralleled the usual designation of the Virgin Mary who was said to excel all women, and this would have rendered easier a conflation of Lady Iveagh and the princes of the Gael in the last two stanzas. We may speculate, accordingly, that such an original version might have sounded like this:

> "Anois mar bharr ar gach mí-ghreann
> chuaigh prionsaí na nGael tar sáil,
> anonn le hainnir na míne
> fuair gairm sa bhFrainc is sa Spáinn -
> anois tá cuallacht ag caoineadh,
> gheibheadh airgead buí agus bán,
> 'siad ná tógfadh seilbh na ndaoine,
> acht caraid na bhfíorbhochtán.
>
> "Aitím ar Mhuire is ar Íosa
> go dtaga siad arís chughainn slán...

"[Furthermore, to top every misfortune, the princes of the Gaels went over the sea; from here for the sake of the gentle maiden they were called away to France and to Spain. Now the populace is lamenting – who used to receive gold and silver. They were those who would not take away the people's possessions, but who were the friends of the very poorest.

> "I beseech Mary and Jesus that they may come safely to us again...]

"It may even be that lines 6 and 44 have become transposed in tradition. If so the conventional description of the Virgin Mary would seem to fit better into the structure of the song, but the lack of evidence of such a transposition from the surviving versions argues against this reading."

Even if it is impossible to ascertain with certainty the original words of the song, it is probable that it is just such a solution (or a variation on it) which lies at the root of the problem with identifying the 'gentle maiden' and her companion. It is only if further early versions of the text come to light that any more definite pronouncement could be made.

Other Compositions Associated with Kilcash

Though *Cill Chaise* remains, and is likely to remain, the best known song of its era to be associated with the area, it is worth noting that it is not the only poetic creation with Kilcash connections. Other Irish compositions include ones we have already mentioned, Ó Rathaille's *Epithalamium for Lord Kenmare* and *The Good Omen*, poems celebrating the marriage of Honora Butler and Valentine Brown.[20] Here, the very fish in the streams and the bees in their swarms celebrate the happy occasion when 'Kilcash has been united lovingly in bonds/With the Prince of Killarney'.[21] *Epithalamium*'s nature imagery and both poems' insistence on the justice of the political order which encompassed families like the Butlers and the Browns is very much of a piece with *Cill Chaise*, as is the apocalyptic imagery specific to *The Good Omen*. This is a picture of life before the fall, and notably the ever symbolic woods are green and vibrant. This was a note which both Ó Rathaille and those who came after him were soon to abandon.

James Hardiman has collected a panegyric entitled *The Lady Iveagh*.[22] Like *Cill Chaise* it too is ascribed to Fr John Lane.[23] However, the poem's apparent confusion about Lady Iveagh's geneaology (a fact we will return to) suggests to us that in its current form at least it was not written by someone who knew her well. Whatever the truth of the matter is, the poem is fairly commonplace in its sentiment and even a superficial glance at it shows it to have been written in a very different vein from that of *Cill Chaise*. For one thing the poem represents Lady Iveagh as still being alive. It has none of the poignancy of the song. Instead, in a conventional manner employing classical references and celebrating unrequited love, Lady Iveagh's great beauty and piety is delineated along with the nobility of her blood and the liberality of her hospitality. Like the subject of so many poems before and since, Lady Iveagh is described as being peerless, the epitome of all the virtues.

In Hardiman the poem is written in the old Irish script and accompanied by a rather stilted and free translation. Dr Tadhg Ó Dúshláine has kindly transcribed it into modern Irish for us as well as providing an English translation.

BANTIARNA IBH(R)EADHACH

Is fada mé ar buaireamh 's gan suairceas 'am dháil,
In arraing gan fuascailt le mór-cheangal grá,
Tré thaitneamh a thabhairt do stuaire na scuabfholt breá,
Ba thriopallach, dualach ar luath-chroith go sáil.
'Si plúr na mban Dhún na mBárc, de chrú na bhfear n-éachtach í,
Siúr ghar don ndiúic-fhear bhí i gcrua-chath na bpilléar í,[24]

Uaisle den dtír í ó Chill Chais an stáit,
A crua-chuaisle dhíreach tá i gcroí mhaith gan cháim.

Is breá deas a féachain, 's a héadan gan teimheal,
'S a dá mhala chaola mar chaomh-tharraing pinn;
A dearcadh breá, réaltach mar chaomh-eala ar linn,
A balsam-ghob chroidhearg 's a déad chailce chaoil;
Is caoin, ceart é a croí geal, gan mhaoímh is is déarcach í,
Príomhcheart gan fíorfhlaith as d'fíorscoth na nGréagach í,
Réilteann na gcúigi, 's í is múinte 's is breá,
Péarla gan siúnta í agus colúr cailce í d'fhás.

Tá spéirbhean bhreá bhéasach ar an dtaobh seo den dtír,
'Sí plúr na mban maorga agus céir na mbeach mín,
Dar thuirling an naomh-spiorad le daonnacht 'na croí,
'Si colúr cailce an tréan fhuil is gan aon chogal tríd;
'S de phréamhcheart na ngroífhear ó fhíor Chaiseal Héabhens í,
Séimhbhean na ndea-bheart de thréanfhuil na laoch mear í,
Phenics tar triúch gur thuirling 'na láimh,
Dá áiteamh mar shampla gur fhág aici an barr.

A lámh mhín ghreanta, néata ar aol-bhrat a scríobhas,
Loingeas ar thréanmhuir agus éanlaith ar chraobh;
Níl cúis maímh ag déithe, 's gur léi le ceart an flíos
Thus Iason mar Aéson 'na chaolbharc thar toinn:[25]
'Sí lonnradh cúig cúigeadh í, 'sí is múinte 's is breá,
Siúr-ghar don diúc-fhear 's do Shúilleabháin Béara í
Iarla ceart Dheasmhumhan a dhearmad ba cháim
'S gach cliar ag teacht chuici ó ghlas Shiúir go Nás.

Tá dhá mhama néata ar a haolbhrághaid bhreá mhín,
'S a píb leabhair, ghléigheal, mar chéadthoradh an droighin.
Tré bhinneacht a béilín do thréig Pan a phíb,
Agus Páris dá mba leis í níor bhaol cath na Troí:[26]
'Sí óg-mhín na n-ógh chaon d'fhóireas ar chléir gach acht
D'ord Chríost' gan mhórphoimp, thréig gach laoch thar lear,
Deirdre an déid ghil gur ghéill dise an barr[27]
I nGael cheart, i ndaonacht, i bhféile 's i gcáil.

Tá mo litir ag dul chugatsa, a údair gach fáigh,
'S más *treason* le scrúdú í, anois umhlaím faoi do láimh;[28]
Ach gur ag trácht ar an státbhean, bhreá, mhánla ba mhian liom a bheith,

'Na mórchuislí dhíreacha mar a scríobhtar 's ea léitear a gceart,
Fite ceartfhuaite ann san mhórfhuil do b'fhearr,
De threabh cheart na rí í do shíolraigh ón Spáinn.[29]
A mbíodh teaghlach chun suite agus slí i ngach ard chuige,
Ag íseal ag uasal ag gruagaibh 's ag fáithe suilt;
Taithí ag gaisgígh bheith ag gleacaíocht le mnáibh
Agus fílí glana líonfa ann dá gcumhdacht gach tráth.

Translation of *The Lady Iveagh*
I'm a long time troubled and happiness is far from me,
In the unrequited pangs of the great bond of love,
Through affection for that beautiful woman with the long flowing hair,
Full-bodied, curly and tumbling to her heels.
She's the pick of the women of Castlehaven, of heroic pedigree,
A close relation of the duke who fought in that terrible battle,
A noble woman from stately Kilcash,
Her proud noble pulse in a stainless heart.

She has a beautiful face, with her classic forehead,
And her two slender eyebrows like the smooth stroke of a pen;
Her lovely gaze, shining like the elegant swan on the lake,
Her sweet ruby mouth and her perfect white teeth;
Her good heart is kind and just, charitable without boasting,
From the noble Grecian race of proud descent
She's the star of the provinces, sophisticated and splendid,
A perfect pearl, the tall slender clear-skinned maid.

There's a fine elegant maiden around these parts,
She's the pick of the noble women and the pure honey of the bees,
The Holy Spirit has descended with charity to her heart,
The pure pillar of the noble line without contamination.
She's from the pure stock of the nobility of Castlehaven
The sophisticated charitable woman of the noble line of heroes,
A phoenix from outside the territory has descended upon her
Proclaiming that she surpasses all.

Her smooth shapely neat writing hand,
Ships on the sea and birds on the branch;
Even gods can't boast, hers is by right the fleece
That Jason, son of Aeson, took in his slender boat across the sea.
She's the light of the five provinces, mannerly and fine,
A close relation of the Duke and O'Sullivan Beare,

The legitimate Earl of Desmond, to forget him would be a mistake,
And every band of poets, from the Suir to Naas, making their way to her.

Two neat breasts on her smooth white bosom,
And her slender white neck is like the first flower of the whitethorn,
Because of the sweetness of her mouth singing Pan abandoned his pipe
And if Paris owned her there would be no danger of the battle of Troy:
She's the gentle young maiden who assists the clergy of every persuasion
Of Christianity without ostentation, who subdued every foreign hero.
(Even) white toothed Deirdre concedes to her the palm,
In Irishness, humanity, generosity and fame.

I'm writing to you, author of every prophet,
And if it's treason to examine it, I submit to your authority;
But to praise that fine, stately, elegant woman is my desire,
In whose noble blood line it is written for all to read,
She is of the finest regal stock descended from Spain.
Room for everyone at her table
Nobility, poor, tramps and jesters
Heroes accustomed to engaging with women
And clear eloquent poets always finding patronage.

It seems to us that the poem's grasp of Lady Iveagh's pedigree seems to be somewhat confused. In the first and third stanzas it is asserted that Lady Iveagh was related to Castlehaven, when of course it was her predecessor at Kilcash, Lady Frances Touchet, who was Castlehaven's daughter (see Chapter II above).

The fourth stanza's reference to O'Sullivan Beare – presumably Donall O'Sullivan Beare (1560-1618), a reknowned military figure who fought at the battle of Kinsale before retiring to Spain where he was created Earl of Bearehaven – is equally puzzling. If Lady Iveagh was related to O'Sullivan Beare, the fact is unknown to us. Perhaps the poet thought that there was some connection through her mother, Helen MacCarthy, the daughter of Donough MacCarthy, the 1st Earl of Clancarthy as the O'Sullivan Beares were originally descended from the MacCarthys, the royal family of Munster?[30]

Having queried this, it was suggested to us by Dr Pádraig Ó Macháin that the text as we have it is a composite one, comprising of an earlier poem which was appropriated by a second, inferior author in order to insert references to a lady from Kilcash.

These intrusions occur in the second four lines of the stanzas in question – only stanza 5 appears to have survived to any degree intact

– and are generally marked by references to the genealogical associations of the person in question.

The result of the intrusions is that the fluidity of the first four lines is interrupted, and infelicities of language and metre are introduced which reduce the whole to a strange looking concoction. This is compounded by the partial repetition in stanza 4 of lines from preceding stanzas: line 5 from st. 2.7 and line 6 from st. 1:6; and by the elongated and mangled appearance of stanza 6.[31]

Learning that we were interested in Kilcash Dr Ó Macháin brought our attention to a poem which we were unaware of, *Cúirt an ghrinn seo Ormond* (*This Pleasure-Court of Ormond*). As we do not know of its having been published elsewhere, we asked Dr Ó Macháin to provide us with an edition of the text and a literal English translation. (A note on its sources and a list of their variant readings is provided in Appendix 4).

CÚIRT AN GHRINN SEO ORMOND

Agallamh idir iníon agus a hathair, noch do thréig a chreideamh do ghrá bídh agus dí Cúirte Chille Caise.

I

Is cailín de shleachtaibh duairc mé 'tá ar fualang trém *Father*,
fear de cheap na suadh, fuair foghlaim agus nós,
le Lúitear go ndeachaigh ar cuaird uainn i gcomhluadar le Sátan
go cúirt an ghrinn seo Ormond, de ghrádh bheith ag ól;
a leabhar gur thréig, 's a phaidrín, 's le bréithribh Dé ní théann a chroí,
's ní mór a spéis in aifreann bhinn Rí gléigeal na gcomhacht,
fios brí na Tríonóide, mo bhrón, liom ní thagrann
ach dom scaoileadh gan choimhdeach i gcoimhdeacht na ndeamhan.

II

A bhruinneall chneasta an tsuaimhnis go luath scuir ded ráitibh:
le Lúitear má chuaigh sluaite go buanghaiste an bhróin
ní rachad leo i gcomhluadar, 's is fuathmhar liom Sátan
do chuir ar dtúis an ársaíocht faoi tháclaí an ghleo;
do thug me seal i n-ifreann saoil, i mbothán deataigh i lúb cois claí,
faoi smúit, faoi thart, ar beagán righis', gan aon ní den só,
's anois ó hoscladh líon dom chun an fhíorsmáilse 'chrothadh dhíom
gan amhras is aoibhinn dom suí scathadh ag ól.

III

A Dhaid mo chroí, mo dhanaid chruaidh an tráth buailfear an truimpéid úd
dod ghlaoch ó leic an tuama go stuamhullach an tsléibhe,
suífidh coiste an Luain ort 's an Mórbhreitheamh taobh leo,
faoi *shentence* tiubhrar daor tú le haonghean don ól;
is fada mé le galar cinn faoi dhoilíos cléibh is osna im chroí
tríd an bhfear dár glaodh mé mar iníon 's ná géillfeadh don ord
do dligheadh chughainn ón Ríoghmhac is fíortheagasc teampaill Chríost,
is do Lúitear an aimhlis ná stríocfaidh go deo.

IV

A iníon chliste an stuaimbhirt, go luath ná tabhair daor mé,
's an Pápa 'na thigh súgaí, gur suanmhar leis beoir,
is fada amach an Luan uaim an buabhall úd a séidfear,
's an barraille go dtréigfidh ní ghéillfead dod ghlór;
is beag mar léan d'fhear bocht dem shlí gan mart chun fóirithin am na dí,
an tart faoi dhó san ló dom chloí, 's mé ag tréigean mo shnó:
ach an *jug* arís má líontar, 's gurb é mo ghlóire saoghail,
's go mbuailfear le clog cling dom, ní stríocfad don ól.

V

Do leas ó léig tú ar cuaird uait ní buan tú insna grásaibh,
tá an saol so ar rith an luasbhirt 's an cruachath fád chomhair;
ach go n-éileoidh an gadaí fuar tú, agus fuagróidh ort báire,
beidh an *jug* 's an crúsca as dáta 's tú sáraithe ón ól;
siúd é an lá ina mbainfear do chling, do scot dá ghlaoch is é gan díol,
do gheall dá dheánadh ag an mBáille Buí 's gan aon urradh id chóir,
beidh *decree* ort friotháilte agus *mittimus* faoi láimh duit
agus Cerberus faoi áthas dod lánghlacadh i gcomhad.

VI

Prionsa an uabhair ná luaigh liom, ná mórmhaistín Sátan,
an Sirriam Buí ná a bháille ní gá liom go fóill,
táid na flaithis fúm ar suíochán i gcúirt an ghrinnse Ormond
's a sailéar súd go dtráfar ní práinn dom gan ól;
sin é féin mo Dhia ar an saol mar a bhfuil cliar dá riar le bia agus fíon,
is ní gairid dóibh ciach ná pianta cinn, daorbhroid ná brón,
an feadh mhairfidh guth nó caint liom is dóibh a dhéarfad mo phaidrín
le fíorghradam cinnte bheith roimhe anns gach ród.

VII

Is measa anois ná riamh tú, is é Dia chuir cúl-lámh leat,
is tharcaisnigh tú an Tiarna thug grian dúinn mar sheoid;
cas anois is iarr Air ód chroí istigh tú a tharrtháil,
ód dhearcaibh sil an áithrí, is gráigh feasta an t-ord;
glaoigh go hard ar chorón na naomh an Mhaighdean mhánla a tháil go fíor
ar Mhac na Páise básaíodh tríot dod shaoradh ó gach smúit,
mar shúil lena cúnamh go bhfaighidh duit na grása arís
chun diúltú don rúnsmáil do thionsgain an t-ól.

VIII

Dá bhfanfainn i bhfad sínte, cloíte, go tréithlag,
blas na dí 's an mhéathmhairt do thréigean tréd ghlór:
na ríochtfhlaithis chímse i gcúirt an ghrinnse Ormond
dob eaglach go mb'fhán dom dá bhfágfainn a mbord;
ní shásaíonn ráite fáidh ná naoimh ná an tsailm ar slánaíodh Dábhí tríd,
ná an t-aifreann Pápa is fearr mar dhlí dár léadh riamh fós
níor bhinne liom leis éisteacht ná an chlingse tá dom ghlaoch chun bídh
go halla ghreanta an aoibhnis seo, m'fhíornós mar ord.

IX

Is déarmhar faoi dhaoirse i gceap tinnte dhuit sáite
an t-aifreann ó cháin tú le sárghean don bhfeoil,
beidh an diabhal is t'aingeal aimhlis id thimpeall dod ghardáil,
is cúirt an ghrinnse Ormond í tráite gan deor;
ó thréig tú Dia 's A chliar ghlan naoimh le grádh don bpiast chuir srian le hÉabh,
beidh ár is ciach is pianta id chroí is tú od shracadh ag leomhan,
beid deamhain 'na saithe od shraoilleadh, 'tabhairt aíocht duit i dteach gan chíos
is t'anamsa dá íospairt ag craoischoin an óil.

X

Do bhreath ná bheart an díoltais lá an daoirse ní gá liom,
ná an phiast dárbh ainm Sátan gé láidir é a chóir,
atá garda sheasta rompu agam i gcúirt an ghrinnse Ormond
d'imreodh an drá leis má tharlaíonn 'na gcomhair;
is é Sparks is Clay 's an séimhfhear Sween, a bhfuil snua na féile ar a n-éadan mín,
atá i gcló na réx le claíomh do chloígh i gCluain Tarbh thíos na Danes,
sin triúr go mba chuí liomsa guí leo le geanas croí,
is feadh do mhairfid ag coimhéad tís dom ní baol dom na deamhain.

Prose Translation of *This pleasure-court of Ormond*
This pleasure-court of Ormond / A dialogue between a daughter and her father, who deserted his religion on account of the food and drink of the court of Kilcash.

I [*Daughter*:] I am a girl of unfortunate parentage, driven to distraction by my father, a man who was of the stock of sages, educated and orthodox, until he left us to journey with Luther, in the company of Satan, to this pleasure-court of Ormond, through love of drinking; he forsook his prayer-book and rosary, and he warms not his heart to the words of the illustrious almighty God, and he has little interest in the sweet Mass of the bright almighty King, he does not, alas, expound to me the meaning of the Trinity, rather he lets me wander unprotected in the company of demons.

II [*Father*:] Fair tranquil maid stop preaching now: if crowds have gone with Luther to the eternal snare of woe, I will not go with them, and I detest Satan who first established wickedness under trappings of war; I was once in a living hell, in a smoky hovel in a recess beside a ditch, depressed, thirsty, with little abundance, without any comfort, and now that I have a chance to throw off this affliction, small wonder I delight to sit drinking a while.

III [*D.*:] Dear Dad, I dread the time when that trumpet will be sounded to summon you from the tombstone to the very summit of the mountain, the doomsday council will sit in judgement on you with the Great Judge beside them, you will be placed under sentence of damnation on account of a singular affection for drink; my head is sick this long time, my bosom distressed and a sigh in my heart, because of the man for whom I was named as a daughter, and who would not respect the religious observance sanctioned by the royal Son with the true teaching of the church of Christ, nor ever part from evil Luther.

IV [*F.*:] Clever resourceful daughter, do not readily condemn me when the Pope is in his drinking house and beer to him a sedative; far away from me is the Judgement Day when that bugle will be sounded, and until the barrel is emptied I will not heed your voice; it is little hardship to a poor man like me not to have a helping of beef at drinking time, to be twice a day slain with thirst, and my complexion waning: but if the jug is filled again, and it to be my earthly glory, until a bell is rung for me I will not desist from drink.

V [*D.*:] Since you have abandoned your wellbeing you will not be in a lasting state of grace, this world is speeding on and the hard battle is ahead of you; but when the cold thief claims you and declares victory over you, the jug and tankard will be useless, you being exhausted from drink; that is the day the bell will toll for you, your fine unpaid and its settlement being demanded, the Yellow Bailiff enforcing a lien on you and you without any guarantor, a decree will be served on you and a mittimus signed for you, and a delighted Cerberus taking you firmly into custody.[32]

VI [*F.*:] Do not mention the Prince of Pride to me, or Satan's great mastiff, neither the Yellow Sheriff nor his bailiff pose any threat to me yet, Heaven is established down in this pleasure-court of Ormond and until its cellar runs dry I will have no need to be without drink; that itself is my earthly God, where poets are served with food and wine, and they are in no danger of anguish, headaches, oppression or grief: as long as I have voice or speech it is to them that I will say my rosary because true and certain honour awaits it everywhere.

VII [*D.*:] You are worse than ever now: God has rejected you, and you have insulted the Lord who gave us the sun as a jewel; turn now and from your heart within ask Him to save you, cry repentance from your eyes and from now on show affection for religious observance; call aloft to the crown of saints for the gentle Virgin, who truly suckled the Crucified Son who was killed on your account, to free you from every stain, in expectation of her help, so that she may obtain again the grace for you to ward off the deceitful sin which led to drink.

VIII [*F.*:] Were I to remain down for long, defeated and feeble, forsaking the taste of drink and fat beef on your advice: I fear I would go crazy if I deserted the table of the heavenly kingdoms which I behold in this pleasure-court of Ormond; the sayings of prophet or saint do not satisfy me, nor the psalm through which David was saved; or the papal mass, officially the best that was ever read, it would not be sweeter to me to listen to that than to the bell-peal which summons me to food, to this decorated hall of enjoyment, my true and customary religious observance.

IX [*D.*:] You will be confined, tearful and captive, in a stock of fire since you have criticised the Mass out of sheer love of meat; the devil and your harmful angel will surround you, guarding you, when this pleasure-court of Ormond will be drained, without a drop of drink; since you have deserted God and His pure host of saints through love of the serpent who entangled Eve, misery, anguish and pains will be in your heart and you being torn by a lion, a swarm of demons will scourge you, lodging you in a rent-free house, and your soul being tormented by the greedy hound of drink.

X [*F.*]: I have no fear of the judgement or act of vengeance on the last day, or of the serpent known as Satan though his power be strong, I have a standing guard against them in this pleasure-court of Ormond who would play a hand with him if they happened to meet him; that is Sparks and Clay and the gentle Sween – the hue of hospitality on their smooth brow – who are like the kings who slew with sword the Danes down in Clontarf, those are three to whom I should rightfully pray with a pure heart, and as long as they mind the house for me I fear not the demons.

Of the two extant sources for this poem only one bears the subtitle which identifies the 'Pleasure-court of Ormond' as Kilcash (see Appendix 4). Apart from this ascription there is nothing in the text which helps to ascertain with certainty the location of the poem. The only references which particularise the poem – the mention of Sparks, Clay and Sweeney in stanza ten – are of no help in identifying it with the area.

Against this we can observe that both sources originate from scribes who lived and worked in the region around Kilcash (see Appendix 4). Dr Ó Macháin has also suggested that this poem's use of *cling* ('bell') calls to mind the bell mentioned in the first stanza of *Cill Chaise*; perhaps there was a bell in the castle grounds whose toll could be heard in the vicinity?

Certainly, the poem might be consistent with what we know of the history of the Butlers of Kilcash in the latter part of the eighteenth century. After the death of Lady Iveagh in 1744 the estate passed into Protestant hands in the person of her son John (d. 1766). After John's death, as we have noted (see Chapter III), Kilcash passes into the hands of the Garryricken branch of the Butler family. John Butler's eventual successor Jack o' the Castle (d. 1795) was also a Protestant and though he was strongly identified with Kilkenny Castle, he was sometimes known as John Butler of Kilcash.[33] We have remarked that these two John Butlers led comfortable lives and the 'pleasure-court' could easily have been associated with either of them.

If the poem is indeed connected with Kilcash it is particularly significant in that it is alone in any way celebrating the castle's Protestant associations. Whereas one might expect that the father would see the 'error' of his ways and return to Catholicism – as the father in other poems in one of the source manuscripts does (see

Appendix 4) – the poem ends with a restatement of his position. Indeed, his last address is interesting in that instead of focusing, as he has done previously, on what might be regarded as essentially hedonistic (plentiful food and drink) qualities, he places his trust in the hospitality and friendship which he has found in the court. In the persons of his comrades these values are perceived as being truly Irish as Sparks, Clay and Sween are identified with the kings who defeated the Viking invaders at the battle of Clontarf.[34]

Father and daughter hold very different theological opinions on the subject of eschatology. At the beginning of stanza three, as elsewhere, the daughter invokes the traditional imagery which was to be found in the *Dies irae* of the Catholic Requiem mass.[35] Her vision of the last things emphasises the judgement of the Great Judge and she expresses herself in the legal language which was introduced with English law (stanza five).

In contrast, the father rejects the fear of judgement or any notions of a divine vengence which might be extracted for his putative sins. Like Oisín – who furnished alternative values to those of St Patrick in earlier Irish poetic dialogues on the relative merits of different religious beliefs – the father presents us with a view-point which draws on imagery just as orthodox as his daughter's. In stanza eight he compares the pleasure-court of Ormond to the table of the heavenly kingdoms thereby recalling the messianic banquet destined for the blessed which is described in Isaiah 25:6, 'a banquet of rich food, a banquet of fine wines, of food rich and juicy'.

The father's refutation of his daughter operates on the level of word choice as well as that of theology. The daughter's bell which tolls for his death in stanza five is negated by the bell of the pleasure-court (stanzas four and eight) which summons him to a laden table. Similarly, the daughter's insistence on the rule of 'religious observance' is countered by the father's religious observance of meal times! (See stanzas three and eight.)

The end result is a carefully poised poem. In the argument of the father the soporific Pope dozing in his drinking house is the butt of some irony (stanza four) and the excessive legalism and fear of some kinds of religious belief are rejected. However, so too are the prophets, the saints and the Penitential Psalms of David (in one of which, Psalm 102, the sinner's only food is ashes while his drink is mixed with tears). This is to go too far as the poet's audience – Protestant or Catholic – would readily have recognised. Presented by the Epicurean father and scolding daughter with two rather extreme positions, the listener or reader sees the wisdom of a middle way and moderation in all things, in food and drink as well as in religion.

The last composition we are aware of which is associated with the vicinity is the eighteenth-century work, *The Blacksmith of Kilcash*.[36] This work also mentions the neighbouring village of Ballypatrick and the townland of Graigue. In form it is a fairly crude ballad which was probably intended to be sung. Hardly a verse goes by without some talk of the happiness associated with alcohol, and in many ways it is an extended masculine fantasy which makes a gesture at political interest only to fall back on the more immediate and pressing questions of the acquisition of the next drink as well as – if the poet is lucky – the company of Nell from Graigue or Tadhg of Bansha's daughter. The attitude of the author is one which was regularly condemned by the clergy of its day and its aspirations are a long way from the lofty virtues praised in various ways in the other literary works we have looked at.

References
1. John O'Daly (1850), 197.
2. Eoghan Ó Néill (1988), 182.
3. We are grateful to Ms Róisín Ní Bhriain of the Irish Traditional Music Archive for bringing this to our attention.
4. There are slight differences between these airs as one would expect from oral transmission. However, the air collected by Petrie is very similar to that to which the song is sung today.
5. Letter of John Dunne to Prim, February 1843, UCDF. Dunne gave the song to John O'Daly, a fact he regretted. A version of the poem was printed by O'Daly in his *Poems and Poetry of Munster*. We also have a manuscript of the song in his hand. See Appendix 3.
6. See Seán Ó Tuama & Thomas Kinsella (1985), 328, 330 and Pádraig De Brún et al eds. (1971), 86-7.
7. See respectively, James Maher ed. (1954), 38; Seán Ó Tuama & Thomas Kinsella (1985), 329, 331 and Brendan Kennelly ed. (1970), 69-70.
8. These appear in the 1920s. See Risteárd de Hae ed. (1939), 168.
9. Daniel Corkery (1979), 35.
10. This may possibly be a reference to the Irish tradition that St Patrick persuaded God to drown Ireland before the world should be consumed by the fire of the apocalypse.
11. Eoghan Ó Néill (1988), 180. For the connection between Kilcash and the Duke of Liria see Chapter III above. The Earl of Castlehaven visited Kilcash before the era of Lady Iveagh (see Chapter II).
12. Ibid., 181.
13. Murray G. H. Pittock (1994), 190.
14. Ibid., 192.
15. Daithí Ó hOgáin ed. (1981), 37.
16. Moray McLaren (1972), 189-191 q.v.
17. See H. A. Doubleday and Lord Howard de Walden eds. (1911-40), X, 161.
18. Daithí Ó hOgáin ed. (1981), 83.
19. Thus John Dunne in a letter of February 1843 [UCDF, Prim Manuscripts].
20. See Aogán Ó Rathaille (1911), 172-5; 232-5.

21. Ibid., 173.
22. James Hardiman ed. (1831), 266-271.
23. See Hardiman's note in ibid., 417.
24. There are a number of possible dukes who would fit this martial description (who is mentioned again later in the poem). Lady Iveagh was related to the first Duke of Ormonde through the maternal line, while her nephew was the Duke of Liria. However, her brother-in-law, the Duke of Berwick is the most likely candidate as his military reputation was well known in Ireland and on the Continent (see Chapter III above). There is also the possibility that the text has misattributed a ducal title to the Earl of Bearehaven mentioned later on in the text.
25. The story of Jason and the Argonauts' peril filled quest for the Golden Fleece is told in Greek mythology. In later tradition the fleece became a symbol of the reward for excellence and endurance.
26. According to Homer's *Iliad* (c. 750 BC) Paris's abduction of Helen was the cause of the siege of Troy. The suggestion is that the lady of the poem surpassed the proverbially beautiful Helen in good looks.
27. Dierdre 'of the sorrows', a figure from Irish mythology, was the daughter of Felim Mac Dall, an Ulster chieftain. Before her birth Cathbad the druid predicted that she would be the fairest woman in Ireland. Like Helen, her beauty was ultimately the cause of a war.
28. Hardiman notes that the author is here submitting his work to the judgement of one of John Clarach Mac Donnell, a Munster poet. [James Hardiman ed. (1831), 417].
29. This, like the earlier reference to Grecian ancestry, is probably poetic embellishment. Otherwise, it may be a reference to the purported relationship between Lady Iveagh and O'Sullivan Beare, who was possessed of a Spanish title.
30. Thomas J. O'Donnell (1960), iv. This may also explain the otherwise puzzling reference – in the following line of the poem – to O'Sullivan Beares being the true Earl of Desmond.
31. Letter to the authors, 24/9/1999.
32. The legal terms 'lien' and 'mittimus' reflect the diction of the Irish text. A lien is a right over another's property held in security against a debt while a mittimus is a warrant committing a person to prison.
33. We think that the possibility cannot be discounted that the 'Pleasure-court' referred to may be Kilkenny Castle under Jack o' the Castle.
34. The battle of Clontarf (1014 AD), where Brian Ború and his Munster allies defeated the Vikings, had been celebrated in poetry since the middle Irish *Cogadh Gáedhel reGallaibh*. It is one of the most famous battles fought in Ireland and thus has a larger symbolic significance.
35. A stanza of the *Dies irae* ('Day of anger') reads: 'The trumpet will fling out a wonderful sound, through the tombs of all regions, driving everyone before the throne [of God].'
36. As an Irish text and notes are readily available in Dáithí Ó hÓgáin ed. (1981), 36-7, 72-3, we have not reprinted it here. The poem was sometimes called *The Blacksmith of Ballypatrick* a fact we infer from a reference by John Dunne to a song of this name in a letter dated 17/12/1866 [UCDF, Prim Manuscripts]. We are grateful to Dr Tadhg Ó Dúshláine (NUIM) for discussing the general context of the poem with us.

Appendix 1: Burials in Cemetery

This is an alphabetical list of those buried in the cemetery which is indexed to the grave numbers of Appendix 2. Where a section is blank, the detail on the headstone was illegible.

...sey	Richard	*Died* 1774	*Grave No.* 61
Anon		*Died* 1730	*Grave No.* 31
Barnes	John	*Died* 1853	*Grave No.* 48
Barnes	John	*Died* 1892	*Grave No.* 49
Barnes	Margaret	*Died* 1799	*Grave No.* 44
Barnes	Mary	*Died* 1786	*Grave No.* 47
Barnes	Mary	*Died* 1855	*Grave No.* 48
Barnes	Mary	*Died* 1873	*Grave No.* 49
Barnes	Samuel	*Died* 1783	*Grave No.* 43
Barnes	William	*Died* 1814	*Grave No.* 47
Brazil	Joan	*Died* 1771	*Grave No.* 18
Brazil	Mary	*Died* 1789	*Grave No.* 18
Brazil	Nicholas	*Died* 1768	*Grave No.* 18
Brien	William	*Died* 1789	*Grave No.* 26
Burk	Richard	*Died* 1774	*Grave No.* 20
Callanan	Rick	*Died* 1781	*Grave No.* 21
Carroll	Edmond	*Died* 1864	*Grave No.* 55
Carroll	Michael	*Died* 1788	*Grave No.* 67
Carroll	Timothy	*Died* 1740	*Grave No.* 67
Clancy	James	*Died* 1780	*Grave No.* 73
Clancy	John	*Died* 1779	*Grave No.* 73
Clancy	Margaret	*Died* 1771	*Grave No.* 73
Clancy	Nelly	*Died* 1783	*Grave No.* 73
Clancy	Richard	*Died* 1778	*Grave No.* 73
Clancy	Roger	*Died*	*Grave No.* 72
Clancy	William	*Died* 1735	*Grave No.* 72
Comerford	Catharine	*Died* 1763	*Grave No.* 76
Comerford	Elizabeth	*Died* 1739	*Grave No.* 76
Comerford	James	*Died* 1691	*Grave No.* 77
Comerford	James	*Died* 1750	*Grave No.* 19
Comerford	Mrs	*Died*	*Grave No.* 19
Comerford	Mrs	*Died*	*Grave No.* 75
Comerford	Ms	*Died* 1763	*Grave No.* 76
Commons	Mary	*Died* 1805	*Grave No.* 3
Commons	Mrs	*Died* 1809	*Grave No.* 3
Commons	Phillip	*Died* 1801	*Grave No.* 3
Comon	John	*Died* 1750	*Grave No.* 19
Costelloe	Catherine	*Died* 1774	*Grave No.* 24
Cummins	John	*Died* 1892	*Grave No.* 4
Dempsey	Ann	*Died* 1793	*Grave No.* 32
Dempsey	Thomas	*Died* 1800	*Grave No.* 34
Denney	James	*Died* 1904	*Grave No.* 65
Denney	James (Jnr)	*Died*	*Grave No.* 65

Donavun	Mary	*Died* 1808	*Grave No.* 15
Donavun	Nance	*Died* 1821	*Grave No.* 15
Dunhy	Edmond	*Died* 1798	*Grave No.* 35
Dunhy	James	*Died* 1814	*Grave No.* 35
Fannin	James	*Died* 1772	*Grave No.* 12
Fannin	Mrs	*Died* 1797	*Grave No.* 12
Garde	James	*Died* 1833	*Grave No.* 1
Garde	Mary	*Died* 1826	*Grave No.* 1
Garde	William	*Died* 1816	*Grave No.* 1
Garmon	Richard	*Died* 1750	*Grave No.* 14
Garmon	William	*Died*	*Grave No.* 14
Gavin	Bridget	*Died* 1986	*Grave No.* 55
Gavin	Helen	*Died* 1958	*Grave No.* 55
Gibbs	Thomas	*Died* 1904	*Grave No.* 39
Gibbs	William	*Died* 1803	*Grave No.* 39
Gorman	John	*Died* 1787	*Grave No.* 13
Griffith	Johanna	*Died* 1887	*Grave No.* 7
Griffith	William	*Died* 1893	*Grave No.* 7
Hackett	Honora	*Died* 1765	*Grave No.* 37
Hackett	Vincent	*Died* 1768	*Grave No.* 37
Hennesy	John	*Died* 1813	*Grave No.* 5
Hennesy	William	*Died* 1813	*Grave No.* 5
Hogan	Bridget	*Died* 1963	*Grave No.* 51
Hogan	Daniel	*Died* 1895	*Grave No.* 36
Hogan	Eleanor	*Died* 1810	*Grave No.* 50
Hogan	Eliza	*Died* 1810	*Grave No.* 50
Hogan	Ellen	*Died* 1963	*Grave No.* 51
Hogan	Francis	*Died* 1976	*Grave No.* 51
Hogan	John	*Died* 1923	*Grave No.* 51
Hogan	Margaret	*Died* 1894	*Grave No.* 36
Hogan	Margaret	*Died* 1896	*Grave No.* 36
Hogan	Mary	*Died* 1807	*Grave No.* 52
Hogan	Nora	*Died* 1982	*Grave No.* 51
Keating	Betty	*Died* 1825	*Grave No.* 30
Keating	Mary	*Died* 1815	*Grave No.* 30
Keily	John	*Died* 1714	*Grave No.* 9
Keily	Richard	*Died* 1741	*Grave No.* 10
Keily	Sarah	*Died* 1741	*Grave No.* 43
Lawlis	Catherine	*Died* 1847	*Grave No.* 60
Lawlis	Pierce	*Died* 1821	*Grave No.* 60
Lawlis	Thomas	*Died* 1853	*Grave No.* 60
Lonargan	Anne	*Died* 1795	*Grave No.* 62
Lonargan	Mary	*Died* 1795	*Grave No.* 62
Lonergan	William	*Died*	*Grave No.* 63
Magrath	Philip	*Died* 1807	*Grave No.* 26
Magrath	Thomas	*Died* 1807	*Grave No.* 27
Mangan	Daniel	*Died* 1826	*Grave No.* 2
Mangan	James	*Died* 1805	*Grave No.* 2
Mangan	John	*Died* 1769	*Grave No.* 2
Mangan	William	*Died* 1817	*Grave No.* 2
Mangen	James	*Died* 1743	*Grave No.* 17

Mangen	Richard	*Died* 1731	*Grave No.* 6
Moffat	Pat	*Died* 1782	*Grave No.* 57
Morrissey	Catherine	*Died* 1717	*Grave No.* 23
Morrissey	Mararet	*Died* 1732	*Grave No.* 23
Morrissy	Catherine	*Died* 1732	*Grave No.* 23
Morrissy	John	*Died* 1734	*Grave No.* 23
Morrissy	William	*Died* 1732	*Grave No.* 23
O'Brien	Brien	*Died* 1758	*Grave No.* 56
O'Donnell	Edmond	*Died* 1918	*Grave No.* 29
O'Donnell	Mary	*Died* 1820	*Grave No.* 38
O'Donnell	John	*Died* 1821	*Grave No.* 38
Phelan	Joana	*Died* 1798	*Grave No.* 45
Phelan	Mary	*Died* 1804	*Grave No.* 46
Pittman	Mary	*Died* 1806	*Grave No.* 74
Power	Jeffry	*Died* 1723	*Grave No.* 16
Roche	Mary	*Died*	*Grave No.* 76
Roche	Mary	*Died* 1762	*Grave No.* 76
Rossel	John	*Died* 1764	*Grave No.* 32
Russell	Margaret	*Died*	*Grave No.* 33
Ryan	Anon	*Died*	*Grave No.* 70
Ryan	Catherine	*Died* 1739	*Grave No.* 67
Ryan	Ellen	*Died* 1774	*Grave No.* 8
Ryan	James	*Died*	*Grave No.* 70
Ryan	James	*Died* 1761	*Grave No.* 8
Ryan	John	*Died*	*Grave No.* 70
Ryan	John	*Died*	*Grave No.* 70
Ryan	John	*Died* 1807	*Grave No.* 59
Ryan	Margaret	*Died* 1764	*Grave No.* 71
Ryan	Mary	*Died*	*Grave No.* 71
Ryan	Mary	*Died* 1809	*Grave No.* 59
Ryan	Michael	*Died* 1770	*Grave No.* 71
Ryan	Michael	*Died* 1793	*Grave No.* 58
Ryan	Philip	*Died* 1752	*Grave No.* 68
Ryan	Phillip	*Died* 1795	*Grave No.* 8
Ryan	Rev. John	*Died* 1824	*Grave No.* 69
Ryan	Thomas	*Died* 1765	*Grave No.* 8
Ryan	Timothy	*Died* 1759	*Grave No.* 8
Ryan	William	*Died* 1796	*Grave No.* 58
Ryan	William	*Died* 1816	*Grave No.* 59
Sextan	Ann	*Died* 1759	*Grave No.* 42
Sexton	Anne	*Died* 1797	*Grave No.* 41
Sexton	Con	*Died* 1809	*Grave No.* 40
Sexton	Laurence	*Died* 1803	*Grave No.* 40
Sexton	Michael	*Died* 1806	*Grave No.* 12
Shea	Judith	*Died*	*Grave No.* 28
Shee	Hon[o]r	*Died* 1750	*Grave No.* 78
Shee	John	*Died* 1740	*Grave No.* 78
Shee	Patrick	*Died* 1740	*Grave No.* 78
Shee	William	*Died* 1749	*Grave No.* 78
Stokes	John	*Died* 1845	*Grave No.* 22
Stokes	Michael	*Died* 1854	*Grave No.* 22

Strang	James	*Died* 1792	*Grave No.* 25
Strang	Joan	*Died* 1757	*Grave No.* 25
Tobin	James	*Died* 1846	*Grave No.* 11
Tobin	John	*Died* 1843	*Grave No.* 11
Tobin	Margaret	*Died* 1961	*Grave No.* 11
Tobin	Peter	*Died* 1949	*Grave No.* 11
Whealane	Margaret	*Died* 1726	*Grave No.* 72

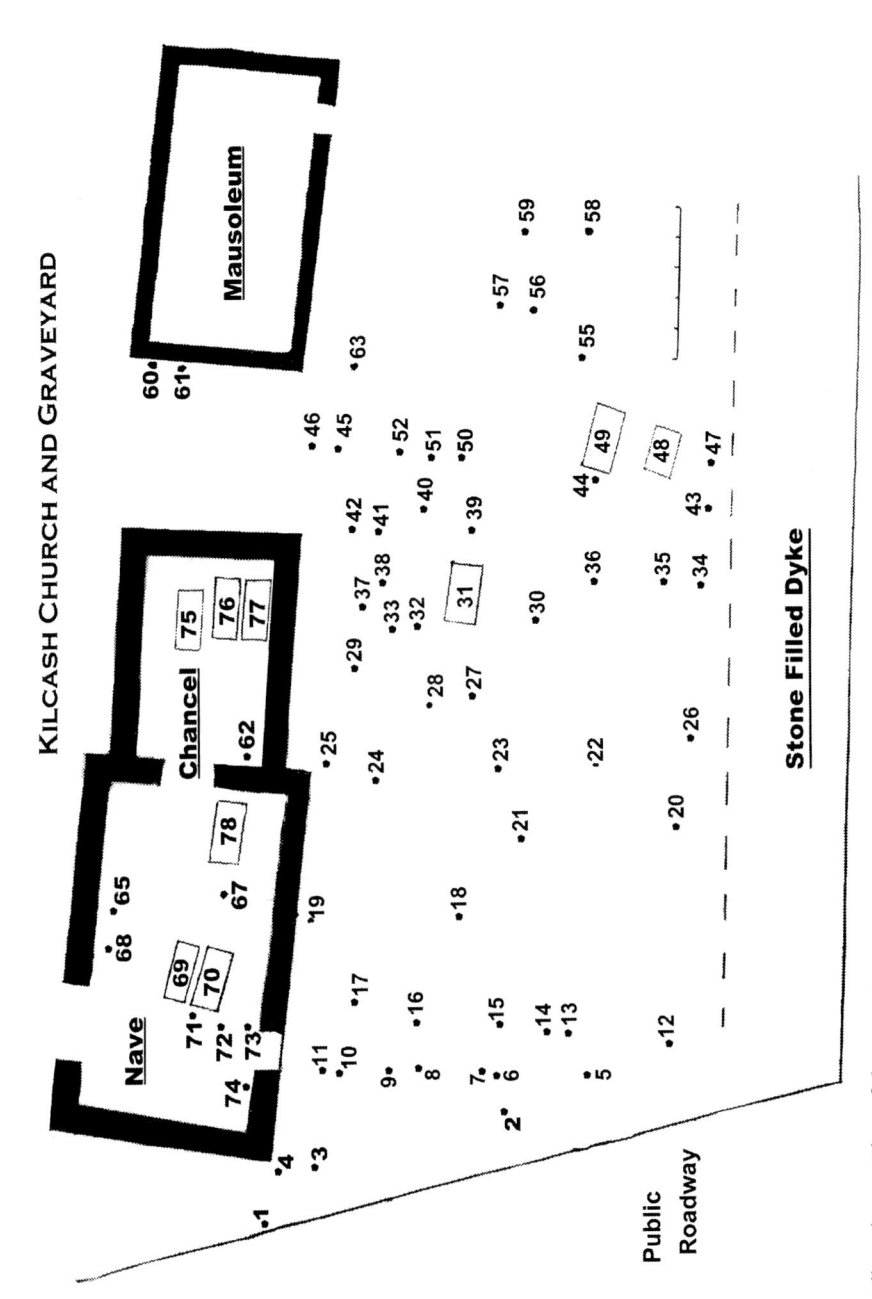

Illus. 4: Plan of the cemetery

Appendix 2: Headstone Inscriptions

The details from the headstones are recorded as they appear in the inscriptions. We have retained abbreviations and unusual or variant orthography with the exception of superscriptions. The physical line breaks on the headstones are indicated by a solidus (/). The numbers correspond to the headstone numbers in Appendix I and in the cemetery map [Illustration 4].

1   Erected to the memory of/Wm Garde of Carrickbeg/who died 23rd of June 1816/Agd 59 yrs & his Wife Mary/Garde alias Ryan who died/20th of March 1826 agd 84 yrs/Also James Garde who died/... of April 1833 agd 20 yrs/and Edward Garde died 20th/of March 1834 agd 18 yrs/Requiescant in Pace Amen

2   Here lies the body of William/Mangan of Ballyknockin who died/Feb. 12th 1817 aged 78 yrs. of his/son James who died Jany 23rd 1805/Aged 27yrs and of his Brother John/ who died May 6 1769 agd/34 yrs May their souls Rest in/Peace Amen Erected by/John & Daniel Mangan of/Ballyknockin/Also Daniel Mangan who died/July 23rd 1826 Aged 47 Years.

3   Erected by John Commons in memory /of his Father Phillip Commons who/depd this life Aug 7th 1801 aged 48 yrs/also his Sister Mary Commons who/dept this life June 23 1805 aged 18/also his Grandmother who depd Oct 21 1809 agd 87.

4   Erected by/Bridget Cummins/of Knockinclash/in memory of/Her beloved Husband/John Cummins/died Jan.29th 1892/Aged 51 years./R.I.P.

5   Erected by Richd Hennesy in Memory/of his Father John Hennesy who/Died March the 26 1813 agd 48 yrs/And Also his Brother Wm who/Died Febr, the 18th 1813 agd 44 yrs/May their Souls Rest in Peace Amen

6   Here Lies y Body of Richd/Mangen who parted this/Life January ye 27 1731 agd 55/Erected by Patrick Mangen

7   In memory of/William Griffith/of Kilsheelan/who died Feb. 5th 1893/aged 67 years/Also his wife/Johanna/who died Sep. 22nd 1887/aged 53 years/Erected by/their Loving children

8   Erected by Matthew Ryan in memory of/his Father James Ryan who depd this life/June the 21st 1761 Aged 53 Years/His Wife Ellen Ryan Als Mahony depd/Novr the 20th 1774 Aged 60 And their /Sons Timothy Ryan July 19th 1759 agd 30/Thos Ryan July 20th 1765 Aged 3l/Phillip Ryan Septr 12th 1795 Aged 67/May they rest in Peace Amen

9   Here Lyeth ye Body/Posterity of John/Keily who decd may ye/16th 1714 Aged 64 years/Also...

10   Here Lies ye Body of/Richard Keily who decd/March ye 12 1741 Agd 52/

11   Erected by Catherine Tobin/of Ballypatrick/in memory of her husband/James Tobin who died/6th August 1846/aged 68 years/Also his brother John/who died 16th Septr.1843/Aged 60 years/Peter Tobin Ballypatrick/died 22nd Aug.1949aged 81 yrs./and his wife/Margaret (Nee Walsh) Died 8th Feb. 1961, aged 81 yrs/May They Rest in Peace Amen.

12   Here Lieth the Body of James/Fannin who died Novbr. the 10th/1772 Agd 65 Yrs Also the Body/of his wife who died Novbr the/8th 1797 Agd 60 Yrs. Also the/Body of Michael Sexton who/died Sep the 11th 1806 Agd 50 Yrs.

13   Here lies the body of John/Gorman who died July 25 1787?Agd 73 yrs/Pray for him

14	Here lies ye Body of/Richard Garmon who/Parted this life February/ye 24th 1750 Aged 35 Also/Wilm Garmon who Parted this life…
15	Here lies The body of/Nance Donavun alias Strang/who died Sber 7 1821 Age 74 Yer/Also Mary Donavun who/Died Sber 24 1808 Age 48/years May their Souls Rest/in peace Amen.
16	Here Lies ye Body of/Jeffry Power Deacd/ye 17th 1723 Agd 42 Yers.
17	Here lies ye Body of/James Mangen who Partd/this life … ye 9…1743 aged/33
18	Here Lies the Body of Nichols/Brazil who Departd this Life/In March 1768 Aged 65 Yrs/Joan Brazil alias Carey Dept./In March 1771 aged 60 years/also the Body of Mary Brazil/Departd this life February the/3rd 1789 aged 17 years.
19	Here lies ye Body of/James Comerford who/Parted this life July ye/27th 1750 Aged 75 years/& his Wife Also John Comon Who Parted this/life August ye 22nd 1750/aged 25
20	Here Lies the Body of/Richard Burk Who De/parted this Life June the/2nd 1774 aged 60/Erected/by his wife Catherine Murphy
21	Here Lies the Body/of Rick Callanan who/Departed this Life 7ber/The 7th 1787 Aged 55….
22	Erected/by Margaret Stokes/ To The memory of her husband/Michael Stokes of Ansforth/who died April 8th 1854/Aged 36 years/Also his father/John Stokes died Feby. 28th/1845. Aged 66 years/May They Rest in Peace Amen/Hogan Clonmel
23	Willm Morrissey Depd this Life/… ye 20 Anno Dom 1732 Agd/73 Yrs his Wife Catherin Dec/ye 1st of April 1717 Aged 45 yrs/Their son John Moresy Dec/April the 25 1734 Agd 35 yrs/Their Daughter Marget Morsy/Dec Aug 13 1732 Ag 27 yrs.
24	Here Lieth the Body of/Catherine Costelloe Wife of William Costelloe who/Depd this Life December/the 14th 1774 aged 40 years.
25	Here lieth the body of James Strang/who depd. this life the 15th of Septr./1792 Aged 75 yrs. Also his Wife Joan Strang als Coftly [?] who depd./this life Decr. the 12th, 1757 aged 28 yrs/Erected by their Son Thoms. Strang/May their Souls rest in Peace Amen
26	Here lieth the Body of/Wiliam Brien, who depd/this life, the 14th of July 1789/aged 27 Years/Erected by his Wife Mary/Brien, alias Fenesy
27	Here lieth the Body of Thos/Magrath of Castletown who/ded. this life June 17 1807 Aged/22Yrs, Also his Father Philip/Magrath of Castletown who/depd. this life Octbr 1807/Aged 80 Yrs.
28	Erected by William Shea/of Garryduff in memory/of his Daughter Judith Shea/who dept. Augst the 20th…
29	In loving memory of/Edmond O'Donnell/Kilnoracy/who died 23rd Sept. 1918/Aged 68 years/R.I.P./Erected by his wife M.A. O'Donnell
30	This Stone Erected by Wm Keating of Carrick-on-Suir in/Memory of his Wife Mary/Keating died Febry the 3rd 1815/Aged 38 yrs. also 4 of his Child/Also his Sister Betty Keating who/died sber the 20th 1825 Aged 41 years/May they rest in Peace Amen
32	Here Lieth the Body of/John Rossel Who De/parted this Life June/the 16th 1764 Aged 87 yrs./the Lord have mercy on his soul.
33	Here Lyeth ye Body of/Margaret Russell deac/ye 23 of March Anno…
34	Here lies the Body/of Thomas Dempsey who depd. this/life Feby, 26 1800 Aged 67 Years/Also his Daughter Ann Dempsey/She died Feby.5 1793 Aged 24/May they Rest in Peace Amen.
35	Here lies the body of James/Dunhy who deped, this life 10th/of July 1814 aged 66 yrs also/his son Edmond deped Novbr/1798 aged 9 yrs/…

36	Erected by/Maryanne O'Donnell/Killonaracy/in memory of Her Parents/Daniel Hogan/who died 16th March 1895/Aged 88 years/Margaret Hogan/who died 13th May 1894/Aged 73 years, /And her Sister/Margaret/who died 13th Jan 1896/aged 32 years/Molloy R.I.P. Callan
37	Here Lieth the Body/of Vincent Hackett/Who Departed this/Life the 25 of Dece/mber 1768 aged 28 yres/also the Body of Honora Hackett/who Departed this/Life the 26 of June/1765 aged 21 Yr.s/Requiescant in Pace Amen
38	Here lie the remains of MARY O'DONNELL/alias Dillon of Kilcash, who departed this life/13th of Feby 1820 aged 74 years also her Husband/John O'Donnell who depd this life 1st of June/1821 agd 101 Yrs. sincerely regretted by their nu/merous friends & acquaintances. Their piety & charity and many pious donations merit the pray/ers of the faithful
39	Erected by/His Dear Parents/in loving memory of/William Gibbs/of Lisronagh/who died 3rd Dec. 1803/aged 30 years/A good nationalist and/Faithful Comrade/Thomas Gibbs/died 4th April, 1904/aged 74 years./R.I.P. Disney, Clonmel
40	Erected by Michael Sexton in/Memory of his father Con Sexton/who departed June the 20 1809/Age 72 Also his Son Laurence/departed February the 12 1803/Aged 33 years
41	Erected by Philip Sexton in/Memory of his wife Anne Sexton/Als Barens She died June the 9th/1797 aged 68 years
42	May ye Lord /God be Mercy/ful to ye soul/of Ann Sextan/who departed/this Life Dece/mber ye 3 1759/Aged 56
43	Here lies ye Body of/Sarah Keily,Allis/Barnes Who Parted/this life May ye 15 1741/Aged 41 Also Samuel/Barnes Who Parted/this life Febry ye 12th 1783/Aged 24 Years
44	Here lieth the body of/Margaret Barnes alias/Walsh who depd. this life/the 18th July 1799 aged...
45	Miss Joana Phelan/departed Septr. 9 1798,/In the 22nd Year of her/Age
46	Erected by Phillip Phelan in memory/of his Mother Mary Phelan (alias/Shanahan) She died Febry the 2d/1804 Aged 70 Years/The Lord have mercy on her Soul Amen
47	Erected by Henery Barns/in memory of his Fathr. Willim./Barnes who depd this life/the 6 of May 1814 aged 70. his wife Mary Barnes alias/Sexton who depd this life/the 13 March 1786 aged 58
48	Sacred To The Memory of/John Barnes/of Graigue who Died July 22 1853/Aged 78 years/Also Mary his wife/who died December 23 1855/aged 66 years
49	In Fond Memory/of/John Barnes/who died August 1st 1892/and of/Mary/his wife/who died March 2nd 1873
50	D.O.M./Erectd, by Danl. & Thom Hogan/of Brenormore in Memory of/their Sisters Eliza Hogan who/depd. this Life, June 10th 1810 Agd/16 Years. Also Eleanor Hogan/Alias Caughlin, who died Augst/the 12th 1810 Agd 29 Years
51	In/Loving memory/of John Hogan/Mullinahone/Died 11th Feb,1923/His wife/Bridget Hoan,/(nee Walsh/Died 12th April 1963/Ellen Hogan (nee Landy)/Died 11th Aug. 1963/Francis Hogan/Died 19 Jan. 1976 aged 76/Nora Hogan,/Died 18 Dec. 1982 Aged 84/R.I.P. Molloy Callan
52	Here lies the Body of Mrs. Mary/Hogan Alias Walsh of Brenormore/who depd. this life the 22nd of Febry,/1807 Aged 37 years/Also...Hogan who depd. this/Life June 12th, 1811 Aged 74 Yrs./Molloy, Callan
55	Erected by/Mary Carroll of Kilcash/in memory of her beloved/Husband Edmond Carroll/who departed this life/November 6th 1864/Aged 78 years/Helen

Gavin/died 25th July 1958/Bridget Gavin/died 14th Sept. 1986/May He Rest in Peace

56　Here Lyeth the Body/of Brien O'Brien Gent/who Depated this life/on Sunday February the 5 1758.

57　Here Lies the Body of Mr. Pat. Moffat/(whose many pious Donations deserve/ the fervent prayers of the Faithful) He/Departed this Life 29th day of June 1782 in the 55th Year of his/Age/Requiescant in Pace.

58　Here Lies the Body of Wilm/Ryan of Ballynacluana who/Departed this Life December/the 30th 1796 Aged 66 years/Also his Son Michael Departd/January the 30th 1793 Age 40

59　Here lies the Body of John Ryan of Ballynaclony/who depd this life the 14 of April 1807 Aged/76 years also his Daughter Mary Ryan who/died Novr 21st 1809 Age 21 Yrs also his Son/William Ryan he died 10th of Nov. 1816 age 26 Yrs/...

60　Erected by Mary Lawlis alias/Strang of Brittas in memory/of her Uncle Thos. Lawlis of Kil-/cash who died 28th Janry. 1853/aged 48 yrs. her Grandfather /Pierse Lawlis of Tour who died /15th Decr. 1821 agd. 75 yrs. also her/Grandmother Cathe. Lawlis/ alias Mangan who died 28th March/1847 aged 97 years/ Requiescant in Pace.

61　Here ly... Body/of Ric...sey/August...1774/Aged 69

62　Here lie the Remains of Mrs. Mary/Lonargan who departed this Life/the 15th of Janry. 1795. Aged 76 Years./Also the Remains of her Daughter/Anne Lonragan who departed this/Life the 9th of March 1795, Aged 28/May the Lord have mercy on their/Souls. Amen

63　Here lies the/body of Will/Lonergan

65　Erected by/Johanna Denney/of Ballypatrick/in memory of her Husband/James Denney/Died 1st Dec. 1904/aged 63 years/His Son James/who died young/R.I.P.

67　Here Lies the Body of Catherin/Ryan who Departed this life in/Decembr. 1739 aged 45 Years also/The Body of Timothy Carroll who/Depd. in ye year 1740 Aged 50 yrs./Michael Carroll Depd. July ye 19th 1788 Aged 27 years

68　Here lies ye Body of/Philip Ryan who Partd/this life April ye 8th 1752/Aged 33 Years

69　Here lie the Remains of the Revd John Ryan/with the true piety & unwearied zeal of the/primitive Apostles he administered the/sacred ries of Religion & feelingly announced the truths of Salvation to his Parishioners of/Ballyneal & Grange over whom presided as Pastor during the period of 15 yrs. in him are/sought [?] exemplified the word of our Devine/Redeemer. I have chosen you & have appo/inted you that you should go & should/bring forth fruit & your fruit should remain/he died in Ballyindony January 16 1824/Aged 50/May his soul rest in peace Amen

70　Here lieth the body of John Ryan late of Bally/nadony who depd this life the 17th of October/...in the...year... Also the body/of...Ryan of Cl...y who depd this life/the...of February.../Also...John Ryan of Ballynadoony/Also James Ryan son of the above John Ryan/who depd this life the...day of Debr.../aged...6.../...

71　Here Lieth the Body of• Mic/Ryan of Ballynaclony Who/Depd this Life October the/15th 1770 In the 73rd year Of/his Age Also His Two dau/ghters Mary Who Depd Nov/the...4 years/Also Margaret Ryan who Depd/June ye 13th 1764 aged 19 Yrs.

72　HERE Lies ye Body/of Margaret Whealane/who Died March the 17th/1726 Aged 50 years/And ye body of her/Son/Roger Clancy/& ye Body of his Father/Willm. Clancy decd. May/ye 1st Agd...

73　Here Lieth the Body of James Clancy/Who Depd this life Decr. the 1st 1780,

Aged/50 Yrs. also his son John Clancy depd. decr./the 10th 1779 Aged 6 Yrs. also his Daughter Nelly Clancy depd. decr. the 21st 1783 also/his Father Richd. Clancy depd. decr. the 22d/1778 Aged 81 Yrs. as also his Mother Margt./Clancy alias Walsh depd. decr. the 22d 1771/Aged 70 Yrs/Erected by his Son Richd. Clancy.

74 Here lies the Body of/Mary Pittman who Depd. this Life the 29th Day of July/1806 Aged 28 Years/May the LORD have mercy on her/Soul Amen

75 Here lies ye body of/...Comerfor/alias Slat...who/departed this life/...aged/42 wife to Edw Com/rford of ...sy/...was/layed...her by/ye order of John/Comerford of K.../resy.../.../.../2 day of...

76 Here lies the body/of Mary Roche.../daughter Elizabeth/Comerford who par/ted this life.../...1739 also the/body of Mary Roche/who parted this life/ the 19 of Dec 1762 aged/46 and daughter/...Comerford who/parted this life the 18 of/Feb 1763 aged 17/and likewise her daughter Catharine Comer/ford who parted this life the 23 of Dec 1763/aged 17.

77 Here lyeth ye body/of James Comerford/late of Kil.../...who.../1691.../also...

78 Here lieth the Body of Patrick Shee of/BallyPatrick who Departed this life 5th of/Novemr 1740 aged 56 yrs his wife Honr/Shee alias Hefernan Departed this life/10th xbr 1750 aged 30 yrs also his Son/William Shee Departed this life 17 7ber/1749 aged 36 yrs also John Shee Depd/this life 20th April 1740 [?] aged 30 years/This Stone was Erected by Michael Shee

Appendix 3: *Cill Chaise* – Textual Notes

This appendix, compiled by Dáithí Ó hÓgáin, accompanies his text of the song *Cill Chaise* which appears in Chapter IV. It lists the source texts of the version printed in Chapter IV and their variant readings. It ends with a note on some of the vocabulary used in the song's composition.

Sources
A   John O'Daly ed. (1850) 196-201: *ll*. 1-56
B   John O'Daly, RIA MS. 12 E 24/47-48 (date c. 1845): *ll*. 1-8, 17-24, 9-16, 41-48, 25-28, 37-40.
C   Nicholas O'Kearney, RIA MS. 23 E 12/97 (date c. 1846): *ll*. 1-56.
D   James Brennan, loose pages in UCDF, Prim Manuscripts (1864). Edited with full variants in Dáithí Ó hÓgáin (1981), 51-2, 81-3: *ll*. 1-18, 21-22, 19-20, 23-24, 41-48, 25-33, 36-34, 37-40, 49-56.
E   John Dunne, loose pages in UCDF, Prim Manuscripts, (1864-1867). Variants cited in Ó hÓgáin (1981), 83-4: *ll*. 1-50.
F   Anonymous, RIA MS 24 C 56/686-88 (second half of 19th century): *ll*. 1-16, 33-40, 25-32, 17-24, 41-56.
G   Broadsheet in National Library of Ireland, no source or date given. From Diarmaid Ó Muirithe (1980), 108-9: *ll*. 1-8, 17-24, 41-42, 49-50, 45-48, 51-56.
H   Anonymous, *Fáinne an Lae* (30/12/1899, 205) : *ll*. 1-8, 17-24, 33-56.

There are also versions collected from oral tradition in the 20th century. Some of these are printed in: Pádraig Breathnach, *Fuínn na Smól* 7 (1913) = Ccól Ár Sinsear (Dublin, 1923), 12-14 [with the air]; Margaret Hannagan & Séamus Clandillon, *Londubh an Chairn* (Oxford, 1927), 17 [with the air]; Liam de Noraidh & Dáithí Ó hÓgáin, *Binneas thar Meon* (Dublin, 1994), 78, 254 [with the air].

The air is also published in the following: Anonymous, *Fáinne an Lae*, (30/12/1899, 205); Charles Stanford, *The Complete Petrie Collection of Ancient Irish Music* (London, 1902-1905), 81, 364; Francis O'Neill, *Music of Ireland* (Chicago, 1903), 18 and *Irish Folk Music* (Chicago, 1910), 338; Patrick Weston Joyce, *Old Irish Folk Music and Songs* (Dublin, 1909), 375.

Variations in Sources
Textual variants from A to H (with orthography standardised, except for dialectal features)

Title: Caoineadh Chille Cais (A)/ Cill Chais (BCG)/ Cill Chaise (DE)/ Coill Chaise (F).
1. créad > cad (EGH).
2. ná a teaghlach > ná ar a teaghlach (BG).
3. níl trácht ar thigh ná ar theaghlach (D)/ níl trácht ar Chill Chaise ná a teaghlach (E).
4. ní bainfear > ní bhuainfidh (C)/ ní bhuailfear (DG).
   a cling > an chling (D)/ an chreill (G).
5. an áit úd a gcónaíodh > Insa bhaile úd a chónaíodh (D)/ an áit úd a gcónaíodh (E)/ ansúd a chónaíodh (F)/ mar is ansiúd a chónaíodh (G).
6. gradam > gairm (ABCDEH).
7. ag tarraing > ag tarraint (D)/ dhá dtarraint (E)/ 'tarraint (F)/ ag tarraingt (G).
   thar toinn > ón bhFrainc (BF) / le taibhse (C)/ fí mheidhir (D)/ le tíos (E).
8. binn > ann (F).
9. is mór an danaoid 'sis léir liom (B)/ is é mo chreach ghéar is mo léanfairt (D)/ 'sé an danaoid is an léir liom (E)/ is mór an dainid agus an léan liom (F).
10. néata > sneachtach (C).
11. an *avenue* ghreanta > is t'aiviní canta (B)/ agus t'*avenue* fada (D)/ an aivine fhada (F).
12. den *walk* > dá mhágh (B) don chuach (C)/ ag fás (D).
13. do chúirt bhreá ná sileadh an braon di (B)/ ná do chúirt bhreá do shileadh an braon di (D).
14. go tláth > ar lár (B).
15. is gur as leabhar na marbh do léitear (B)/ i leabhar na marbh a léitear (C)/ is as leabhar na marbh do léimid (D)/ is as leabhar na marbh ní léitear (E)/ gur as leabhar na marbh a léadh siad (F).
16. ár n-Easpag ná *Lady Iveagh* (E)/ ar an éaspag is *Lady Iveagh* (F).
17. ní chluinim > ní chloisim (CEG)/ ní chloisfear (D)/ is ní airím (F).
    fuaim lacha ná gé > fuaim lachan ná géí (A)/ glór lachan ná géanna (B)/ ceol lachan ná géanna (DG).
18. ná an fiolar ag déanamh faire ar chuan (D)/ ná fiolar ag déanadh aeir ar chuan (F)/ ná fiolar ag déanamh ar chuan (G)/ ná fiolair ag éamh chois cuain (H).
19. ná fiú na beacha a dhéanfadh saothar (D).
20. a thabharfadh > a thugadh (D)/ bheireadh (F).
21. ná glór binn blasta na n-éan ann (B)/ nó ceol binn milis na n-éan ann (C)/ ná an smóilín binn milis na gcraobh ann (D)/ ná ceol binn canta na n-éan ann (F).
22. le hamharc an lae a bhreith uainn (BE)/ ar ghluaiseadh an lae

bhreá uainn (C)/ ar amharc an lae is an Luain (D)/ ar amharc an lae a bhreith uainn (FG)/ le hamharc an lae ag dul uainn (H).
23. i mbarra na ngéag > ar bharra na géige (D)/ ar bharraí na gcraobh (G).
24. ó, 'sí a chuirfeadh > do chuirfeadh (D).
   chum suain > fá shuairc (F).
25. a thigeann > thigeadh (A)/ thig (C)/ a théann (BDEF).
   faoi na > fí sna (D).
26. is a gcoin lena dtaobh chum scíth (B)/ le gunna lena dtaobh as líon (C)/ agus na gadhair lena dtaobh is ina líon (D)/ lena ngunna lena dtaobh sa tír (E)/ a gcoin lena dtaobh sa líon (F).
27. anuas le léan ar > uathu ó sna maolchnoic (B)/ síos go léanmhar (D)/ uathu le léan air (F).
28. *sway* in gach tír > só ins gach tír (B)/ céim gach tír (C).
29. an fhaiche bhreá aoibhinn 'na raobthacha (A)/ an áit bhreá aoibhinn ina réabacha (C)/ tá an t-áitreabh greanta so réabtha (D)/ an áit bhreá briste ina réabacha (E)/ thá an áit bhreá briste réabtha (F).
31. an pháirc is na mágha réabtha (C)/ tá an pháirc an *phaddock* ina *dairy* (D)/ is páirc an phaidic faoi shaothar (F).
32. mar a mbíodh > in áit (DF).
33. atá ceol-néall trom ar chraobhaibh ann (C)/ tá ceo fí bhrataibh ón spéir ann (D)/ thá ceo ag titim ar chraobhacha ann (E)/ dén smúit seo ag titim ar chraobhacha (F)/ tá ceo ag titim ar chraobh ann (H).
34. ná tirimíodh gaoth ná lá (F).
   grian > gréin (DH).
35. tá ceo agus brataibh ón spéir ann (F).
36. is an t-uisce go léir i dtrá (C)/ is a cuid uisce d'éalaigh ar trá (D)/ agus gainimh ag séideadh air tráth (F).
37. níl caora ann > ná craobh ann (D)/ níl caor ann (H).
38. maolchlocháin > maolchlaíocháin (BDF).
39. páirc na foraoise > páirc an fhoraois (A)/ is tá páirc an *chover* (B)/ is tá páircín na *covers* (D)/ thá páirc an *cover* (E)/ agus páirc an *chover* (F)/ páirc an fhoraoise (H).
40. is d'imigh an *game* chum fáin > ó dh'imigh i gcéin chum fáin(B)/ is do dh'imigh an *game* le fán (D)/ is d'imigh an *game* chún fáin (E).
41. Anois mar bharradh ar gach ní dhíobh (D)/ agus súd mar bharr ar gach aon ní (F)/ Anois ó chuaigh ainnir na mínchrobh (G).
43. ag triall ar bhruinneall na míne (B)/ chuaigh le hainnir méin mhaith (F)/ le taitneamh dá maoin thar sáil (G).
44. 'fuair gairm thar mhílte mná (B)/ 'fuair gairm thar mhílte 'e mhná (D)/ fuair gradam thar na mílte mná (F).

45. anois tá > is buartha athá (B)/ is dubhach 'tá (D)/ is buartha a bhí (F).
    dá caoineadh > ga caoineadh (C)/ ag caoineadh (F).
46. gheibheadh > a fhaigheadh (D)/ fuair (F).
47. is níor thóg sí riamh seilbh na mbaintreach (B)/ 'sí nár bhain a raibh 'e sheilbh de bhaintreach (D)/ 'sí ná tógadh seilbh na ndaoine ann (E)/ níor thóg riamh seilbh na maoine (F)/ níor bhain riamh seilbh de bhaintreach (G).
48. ach caraid > ach cara (C)/ is í an cara (D)/ aon charaid (E)/ is tú cara (G).
49. aitím ar Mhuire is ar Chríost (C)/ tá mo shúilse le Muire agus le hÍosa (D)/ thá mo shúilse trí Mhuire le hÍosa (F)/ iarraimse ar Mhuire is ar Íosa (G).
50. go bhfillfidh sí aríst chughainn slán (D)/ go dtiocfadh arís chughainn slán (F).
51. go mbeadh rince fada ag góil thimpeall (D)/ go mbeadh rincí fada ag gabháil thimpeall (F).
52. veidhlín > *fiddles* (D)/ *fiddle* (F).
    tinte > tintí (D).
53. go dtógfaimist baile breá sinsir (D)/tógfaimid baile breá sinsir (F).
54. i gCill Chaise seo thíos go hard (D)/ i gCoill Chaise so thiar go hard (F)/ Cill Chais seo thíos go hard (G).
55. is go brách nó go dtiocfaidh > is go brách go dtiocfas (D)/ agus go deo go dtiocfadh (F)/is go brách nó go dtiocfadh (G).
56. ní fheicfear > ní fheicfí (G)/ ná feicfear (H).
    í arís > aríst é (D).

A Note on Vocabulary

Some features which occur suggest composition by a literary author, rather than a folk author who had picked up some literary traits. These features are listed here, with the spoken variants in the Irish dialect of the area in brackets: créad (cad); tá (thá); ní bainfear (ní bhainfear); bráth (brách); níl (nín); ina gcónaíodh (a gcónaíodh); tar (thar); tarraing (tarraint); faoi (fí); ní chluinim (ní chloisim/ ní airím); fiú na mbeacha – dialectal 'fiú na meacha' (fiú na mbeach); chum (chún); a thig[eann] (a thagann); faoi na sléibhte (fí sna sléibhte); gabháil (góil); timpeall (thimpeall); arís (aríst); acht (ach).

On the other hand, some more dialectal forms indicate that the composer did not adhere absolutely strictly to literary usage. These instances (with literary forms in brackets) are: a sileadh (na sileadh); in leabhar (i leabhar); déanadh (déanamh).

Appendix 4: *Cúirt an ghrinn seo Ormond* – Textual Notes

This appendix, compiled by Pádraig Ó Macháin, accompanies his edition of the poem *Cúirt an ghrinn seo Ormonde* which appears in Chapter IV. It lists the source texts of the version printed in Chapter IV and their variant readings.

Sources
R: RIA MS. 552 (23 L 10) pp. 273-6 (scribe: Thomas Meagher, Croan, Co. Tipperary, and Killamory, Co. Kilkenny, 1833-5).

G: NLI MS. G 403 pp. 268-71 (scribes: Tomás Ó hÍceadha with Gearóid Ó Maonaigh, Waterford, 1845—9, this text being dated 28 February 1845).

The heading identifying *Cúirt an ghrinn seo Ormond* as Kilcash is found only in G.

The scribes of these manuscripts were both familiar with the neighbourhood of Kilcash. Croan, one of the addresses of Thomas Meagher, scribe of R, is a townland roughly six miles north-east of Kilcash, and borders Killamory in Co. Kilkenny. Tomás Ó hÍceadha, a well-known and prolific scribe from Graystown near Killenaule, wrote material in 1819 and in the 1820s for Séamas Ó Meára of Clonmel, eight miles south of Kilcash.

In general, G is superior to R; and the text of G is followed here. That both scribes were drawing on related source-material is demonstrated by the number of other texts shared between the two manuscripts.

In R our poem is followed (pp. 277-301) by a series of poems - entitled 'An teagasc órdha' - not present in G, in which a daughter ('Neil óg') upbraids her father (apparently one Séamas Ó Faoláin) for deserting 'ord na n-aspal' in favour of 'ord na Saxon', specifically 'le grá don só bhídh ar bhord an halla'. The repentant father details how he has, one by one, broken all the Commandments, and the sequence concludes with his poem of penitence.

In addition to sharing the basic premise of our poem, this series of poems contains a number of verbal echoes of *Cúirt an ghrinn seo Ormond*. This suggests that the series may have been composed as a sequel to the *Cúirt,* and perhaps as a corrective to its celebration of the profanity of Kilcash. Both poems may well have been composed by the same poet.

Variations in Sources

I 1 an dúairc R; 1 fuathlan G, fúadhlan R; 2 suaidh G; 5 bréithribh] athanta R; 5 théitheann G, theibhin R; 6 bhinn *om.* R; 8 ccuimhdeacht G.

II 2 buanghaiste] búan tráp R; 4 do chuir] a cheap R; 4 ársuigheacht GR (= *arsaidheacht* 'military prowess', with influence of *aidhbhirseoireacht*?); 5 lúib G; 6 righis] (< raidhse, rairdhse, rírdhse?) ríos R; 8 aimhrios G.

III 1 mo dhanaid] m'aicíd R; 4 tiubhrar] tábharfar R; 5 osna] fearta R; 6 dár] 'nar R; 8 do] le R.

IV 1 Anghir R; 3 an tráth buaillfar a trumpéid úd R; 6 shnuaidh G; 7 is fíor gurb é R; 8 o'n ol R.

V 2 luasbert G; 3 fuair GR; 5 *sic* R, do sgot gan díol agus í dá glaodhach G; 7 faoi láimh duit] le peannda a sgríobh R; 8 ccoimhead G.

VI 3 fúm] rómsa R; 5 mar atá R; 6 nach geárradh…a ndaor-bhruid fa bhrón R; 7 guith G.

VII 3 anois] go crinn R; 3 ó iachdar do chroidhe pardun R; 5 glaodh G; 7 chongnamh…ffuighid G; 8 ur-small R.

VIII 2 dá ttréiginn R; 8 ghrannda R.

IX 3 aimhlis] cuídeacht R; 5 chliar ghlan] chliaracht R; 5 hÉibh G; 7 aíocht] tíos R.

X 3 rompu] roimhe R; 4 dimireochadh G; 6 Rakes R; 6 do chlaoidh na Danes a gClúain-tóir R; 7 go mba chuí] ó! Mo chuimh*idh* G, a ma chuidhe R.

Genealogy of the Butlers of Kilcash

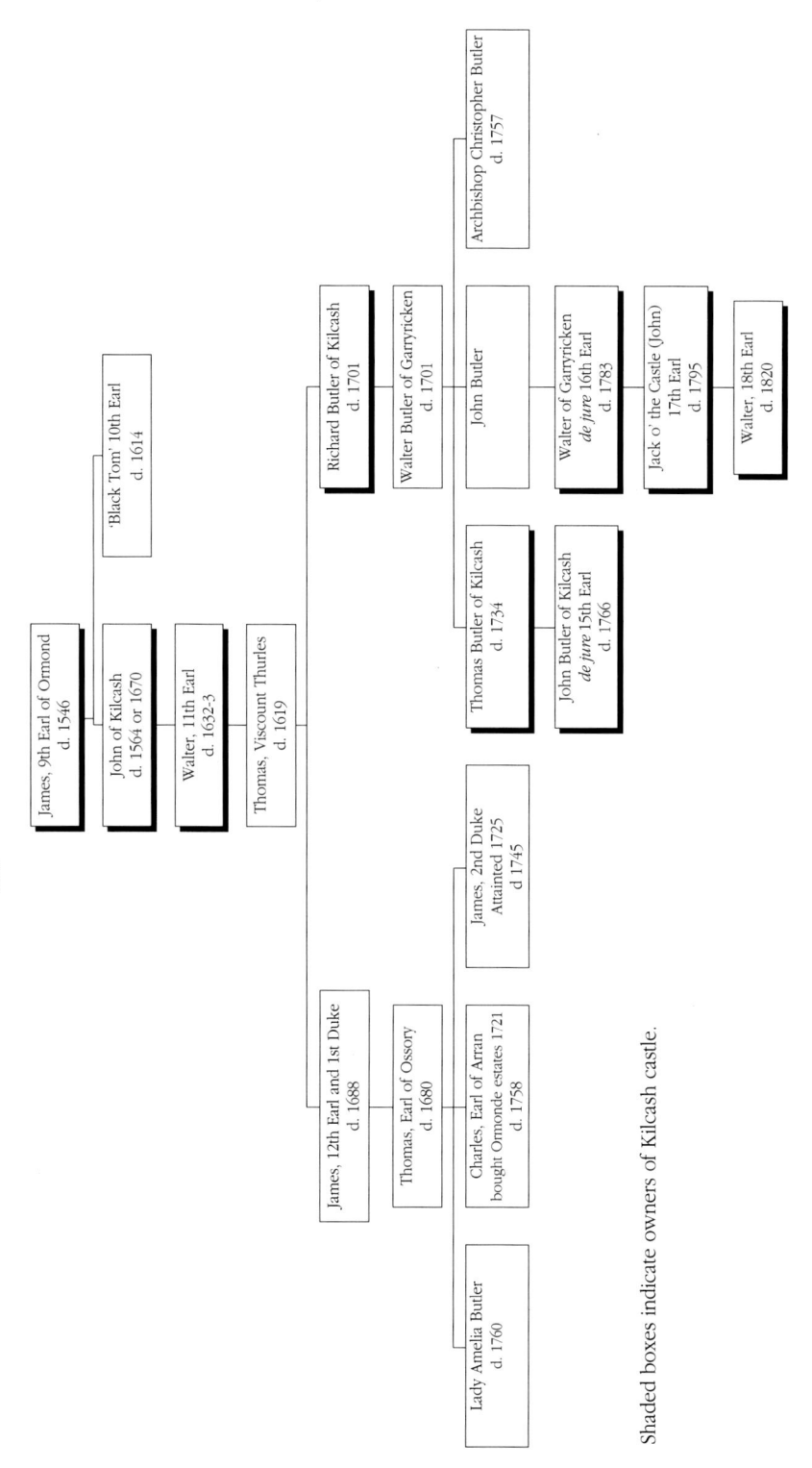

- James, 9th Earl of Ormond
  d. 1546
  - 'Black Tom' 10th Earl
    d. 1614
  - John of Kilcash
    d. 1564 or 1670
    - Walter, 11th Earl
      d. 1632-3
      - Thomas, Viscount Thurles
        d. 1619
        - James, 12th Earl and 1st Duke
          d. 1688
          - Thomas, Earl of Ossory
            d. 1680
            - James, 2nd Duke
              Attainted 1725
              d 1745
            - Charles, Earl of Arran
              bought Ormonde estates 1721
              d. 1758
              - Lady Amelia Butler
                d. 1760
          - Richard Butler of Kilcash
            d. 1701
            - Thomas Butler of Kilcash
              d. 1734
            - John Butler of Kilcash
              de jure 15th Earl
              d. 1766
          - Walter Butler of Garryricken
            d. 1701
            - John Butler
              - Walter of Garryricken
                de jure 16th Earl
                d. 1783
                - Jack o' the Castle (John)
                  17th Earl
                  d. 1795
                  - Walter, 18th Earl
                    d. 1820
          - Archbishop Christopher Butler
            d. 1757

Shaded boxes indicate owners of Kilcash castle.

Bibliography

MANUSCRIPT SOURCES
Council MS. – Environmental Section, South Tipperary County Council.
Dúchas MS. – Department of Arts, Heritage, Gaeltacht and the Islands, Dublin.
NLI – National Library of Ireland, Manuscript Reading Room.
Registry MS. – Registry of Deeds, Dublin.
RIA – Royal Irish Academy, Dublin.
Skehan Papers – Skehan Papers, St Patrick's College, Thurles, Co. Tipperary.
TCD – Trinity College, Dublin, Manuscripts Department.
Thurles MS. – County Library, Thurles, Co. Tipperary.
UCDF – Department of Irish Folklore, University College, Dublin.

PRINTED SOURCES
Primary Sources
Atkinson, Ernest George ed. (1895). *Calendar of the State Papers Relating to Ireland Preserved in the Public Records Office, January 1598-1599 March.* London: HMSO.
Bliss, W. H. ed. (1893). *Calendar of Entries in the Papal Registers Relating to Great Britain and Ireland. Volume 1. 1198-1304.* London: HMSO.
Castlehaven, Earl of (1815). *The Earl of Castlehaven's Memoirs; or, his Review of the Civil Wars in Ireland.* Ed. P. Lynch. Dublin: Espy and Cross.
Census of Ireland: General Alphabetical Index to the Townlands and Towns, Parishes, and Baronies of Ireland. (1861) Dublin: Alexander Thom.
Chaucer, Geoffrey (1990). *The Riverside Chaucer.* 3rd ed. Ed. Larry D. Benson. Oxford: Oxford University Press.
Clare, Wallace ed. (1932). *The Testamentary Records of the Butler Families in Ireland.* Peterborough: Peterborough Press.
Cobbet's Complete Collection of State Trials, 1627-1640 (1809) Vol. 3. London: R. Bagshaw.
Curtis, Edmund ed. (1932-43). *Calendar of Ormond Deeds.* 6 vols. Dublin: The Stationery Office.
Danaher, K. and J. G. Simms eds. (1962). *The Danish Force in Ireland 1690-1691.* Dublin: Irish Manuscripts Commission.
Davidson, L. S. & J. O. Ward eds. (1993). *The Sorcery Trial of Alice Kyteler.* Binghamton, New York: Medieval & Renaissance Texts & Studies.

De Brún, Peadraig et al eds. (1971). *Nua-Dhuanaire I.* Dublin: Institiúid Árdléinn Bhaile Átha Cliath.

Fagan, Patrick ed. (1995). *Ireland in the Stuart Papers: Correspondence and Documents of Irish Interest from the Stuart Papers in the Royal Archives, Windsor Castle.* 2 vols. Dublin: Four Courts Press.

Gilbert, J. T ed. (1971). *A Jacobite Narrative of the War in Ireland 1688-1691.* Shannon: Irish University Press.

Gilbert, J. T. ed. (1882-1891). *History of the Irish Confederation and the War in Ireland, 1641-43.* 7 vols. Dublin: M. H. Gill & Son.

Griffith, M. C. ed. (1966). *Irish Patent Rolls of James I.* Dublin: Irish Manuscripts Commission.

Hamilton, Hans George ed. (1860). *Calendar of the State Papers Relating to Ireland Preserved in the Public Records Office, 1509-1573.* London: Longman, Green, Longman & Roberts.

Hardiman, James ed. (1831). *Irish Minstrelsy.* Vol. 2. London: Joseph Robins.

Historical Manuscripts Commission (1895-1912). *Calendar of the Manuscripts of the Marquis of Ormonde, K.P. Preserved at Kilkenny Castle.* New Series, 7 vols. London: HMSO.

Historical Manuscripts Commission (1905). *Report on the Manuscripts of the Earl of Egmont.* Vol. 1. London: HMSO.

Historical Manuscripts Commission (1906). *Report on Franciscan Manuscripts Preserved at the Convent, Merchants' Quay, Dublin.* Dublin: HMSO.

Hogan, James ed. (1936). *Letters and Papers Relating to the Irish Rebellion Between 1642-46.* Dublin: Stationery Office.

Hogan, Richard (1744). *A Funerall Sermon on the Right Honourable, Lady Margaret Burk, of Clanrickard; Viscountess Iveagh: Late Relict of the Honourable Colnel Thomas Butler, of Killcash.* Waterford: Jer. Calwell.

Hogan, Richard (1754). *A Funerall Sermon, on The Most Illustrious Christopher Butler, A. B. of Casshel, &c.* Waterford: J. Calwell.

Holland, Patrick (1983). *Tipperary (S.R.) Sites, Monuments, and Artefacts Record.* N.p.

John O'Donovan (1930/1840). 'The Parish of Kilcash' in Michael O'Flanagan ed. *Letters Containing information relative to the Antiquities of the County of Tipperary Collected during the Progress of the Ordnance Survey in 1840.* Vol. 1. Bray: n.p.

Kavanagh, John ed. (1932-1949). *Commentarius Rinuccinanus De Sedis Apostolicae Legatione Ad Foederatos Hibernios Catholicos Per Annos 1645-1649.* 6 vols. Dublin: Stationery Office.

Kennelly, Brendan ed. (1970). *The Penguin Book of Irish Verse.* Harmondsworth: Penguin Books.

Laffan, Thomas ed. (1911). *Tipperary's Families: Being the Hearth Money Records for 1665-6-7.* Dublin: James Duffy & Co.

Lart, C. E. Ed. (1910). *The Parochial Registers of Saint Germain-en-Laye: Jacobite Extracts of Births Marriages and Deaths.* Vol. 1. London: St Catherine Press.

Mahaffy, Robert Pentland ed. (1903). *Calendar of the State Papers Relating to Ireland Preserved in the Public Records Office, 1647-1660.* London: HMSO.

Mahaffy, Robert Pentland ed. (1905). *Calendar of the State Papers Relating to Ireland Preserved in the Public Records Office, 1660-1662.* London: HMSO.

Mulloy, Sheila (1983-84). *Franco-Irish Correspondence, December 1688-February 1692.* 3 vols. Dublin: Irish Manuscripts Commission.

Ó hÓgáin, Dáithí ed. (1980). *Duanaire Osraíoch.* Dublin: Clóchomhar.

Ó hÓgáin, Dáithí ed. (1981). *Duanaire Thiobraid Árann.* Dublin: An Clóchomhar.

Ó Muirithe, Diarmuid (1980). *An tAmhrán Macarónach.* Dublin: Clóchomhar.

Ó Rathaille, Aogán (1911). *Dánta Aodhagáin Uí Rathaille.* 2nd ed. Patrick S. Dinneen & Tadhg O'Donoghue eds. London: Irish Texts Society.

Ó Rian, Pádraig ed. (1985). *Corpus Genealogiarum Sanctorum Hiberniae.* Dublin: Dublin Institute for Advanced Studies.

Ó Tuama, Seán & Thomas Kinsella (1985). *An Duanaire 1600-1900: Poems of the Dispossessed.* Portlaoise: Dolmen Press.

O'Byrne, Eileen ed. (1981). *The Convert Rolls.* Dublin: Irish Manuscripts Commission.

O'Daly, John ed. (1850). *The Poets and Poetry of Munster: A Selection of Irish Songs by the Poets of the Last Century.* 2nd ed. Dublin: John O'Daly.

O'Donovan, John ed. (1990/1636). *Annals of the Kingdom of Ireland, by the Four Masters.* 3rd ed. Dublin: De Búrca Rare Books.

O'Donovan, John trans. (1864, 1630). *The Martyrology of Donegal: A Calendar of the Saints of Ireland.* Ed. James Henthorn Todd & William Reeves. Dublin: Irish Archaeological and Celtic Society.

O'Flanagan, M. ed. (1930/1840). *Ordnance Survey Name Books – Co. Tipperary from Gaile to Kilgrant.* N.p.

Parliamentary Gazetteer of Ireland, 1846. Vol. 5. Dublin and London: A. Fullerton & Co.

Paul of St Ubald (1654). *Iesus, Maria, Joseph, Teresia: The Soul's Delight.* Antwerp: William Lesteens.

Pender, Séamus (1939). *A Census of Ireland c. 1659.* Dublin: Stationery Office.

Petrie, Charles ed. (1951). *The Duke of Berwick and his son: some unpublished letters and papers.* London: Eyre & Spottiswoode.
Simington, Robert C. ed. (1931). *The Civil Survey AD 1654-56: County of Tipperary Vol 1.* Dublin: Stationery Office.
St John Brooks, Eric ed. (1936). *Register of the Hospital of S. John the Baptist.* Dublin: Stationery Office.
Stout, Geraldine et al. (1992). *Sites and Monuments Record; County Tipperary South Riding.* Dublin: OPW.
Sweetman, H. S. (1886). *Calendar of Documents Relating to Ireland 1302-1307.* Vol. 5 of series. London: Longmans & Co.
Tate, Lilian ed. (1959). *Analecta Hibernica No 21: Franco-Irish Correspondence December 1688-August 1691.* Dublin: Irish Manuscripts Commission.
Taylor and Skinner (1783). *Maps of the Roads of Ireland.* Dublin: Wilson and Allen.
The Irish Fiants of the Tudor Sovereigns (1994). 4 vols. Dublin: Éamonn de Búrca.
White, Newport B. ed. (1932). *The Red Book of Ormond.* Dublin: Stationery Office.
White, Newport B. ed. (1936). *Irish Monastic and Episcopal Deeds, AD 1200-1600.* Dublin: Stationery Office.
White, Newport B. ed. (1943). *Extents of Irish Monastic Possessions 1540-1541.* Dublin: Stationery Office.
William M. Hennessy et al. eds. and trans. (1887-1901). *The Annals of Ulster.* 4 vols. Dublin: HMSO.
Wright, Thomas ed. (1843). *Narrative of the Proceedings against Dame Alice Kyteler for sorcery. Camden Society Publications no. 24.* London: Camden Society.
Yeats, W. B. (1992). *The Poems.* Ed. Daniel Albright. London: Everyman's Library.

Secondary Sources and Reference Works

Barry, T. B. (1987). *The Archaeology of Medieval Ireland.* London and New York: Routledge.
Barry, T. B. (1993). 'Late Medieval Ireland: Social and Economic Transformation, 1350-1550' in B. J. Graham and L. J. Proudfoot eds. *An Historical Geography of Ireland.* London & San Diego: Academic Press.
Beckett, J. C. (1990). *The Cavalier Duke: A Life of James Butler – 1st Duke of Ormond.* Belfast: Pretani Press.
Bigger, Francis Joseph (1909). *Irish Penal Crosses 1713-1781.* Belfast: W. & G. Baird Ltd.
Bric, Maurice (1985). 'The Whiteboy Movement, 1760-1780' in William

Nolan, ed. *Tipperary: History and Society. Interdisciplinary Essays on the History of an Irish County*. Dublin: Geography Publications.

Burghclere, Lady (1912). *The Life of James First Duke of Ormonde, 1610-1688*. 2 vols. London: John Murray.

Burke, Thomas (1762). *Hibernio Dominicana*. Coloniae Agrippinae, ex Typographia Metternichiana sub Signo Gryphi.

Burke, W. P. (1894). 'Local Church Architecture from the 12th to the 15th Century – Kilcash'. *Journal of the Waterford and South East of Ireland Archaeological Society*. (1) pp. 265-267.

Burke, William (1983, 1907). *History of Clonmel*. 2nd ed. Kilkenny: Roberts Books.

Burke's Peerage and Baronetage. (1980) 105th ed. 4th impression. London: Burke's Peerage (Genealogical Books) Ltd.

Butler, William F. (1929). 'The Descendants of James, Ninth Earl of Ormond'. *Journal of the Royal Society of Antiquaries of Ireland* (69:1), pp. 29-44.

Cairns, C. T. (1987). *Irish Tower Houses: A Co. Tipperary Case Study*. Athlone: Group for the Study of Irish Historic Settlement.

Cairns, Conrad T. (1994). 'The Tower Houses of County Tipperary', 2 vols. Unpublished PhD thesis, Trinity College, Dublin.

Carrigan, William (1905). *The History and Antiquities of the Diocese of Ossory*. Vol. 4. Dublin: Sealy, Bryers & Walker.

Carte, Thomas (1851/1735-6). *The Life of James Duke of Ormond; Containing an Account of The Most Remarkable Affairs of his Time, and Particularly of Ireland under his Government*. New Ed. 4 vols. Oxford: At the University Press.

Cohn, Norman (1975). *Europe's Inner Demons: An Enquiry Inspired by the Great Witch-Hunt*. London: Heinemann.

Connolly, S. J. ed. (1998). *The Oxford Companion to Irish History*. Oxford: Oxford University Press.

Coonan, Thomas L. (1954). *The Irish Confederacy and the Puritan Revolution*. Dublin: Clonmore & Reynolds Ltd.

Corkery, Daniel (1979). *The Hidden Ireland: A Study of Gaelic Minstery in the Eighteenth Century*. Dublin: Gill & Macmillan. 1st published 1924.

Crawford, E. Margaret ed. (1989). 'William Wilde's Table of Irish Famines, 900-1850' in E. Margaret Crawford ed. *Famine: The Irish Experience 900-1900*. Edinburgh: John Donald Publishers Ltd.

Cressy, David (1997). *Birth, Marriage and Death: Ritual, Religion, and the Life-Cycle in Tudor and Stuart England*. Oxford: Oxford University Press.

Crookshank, Anne (1986). 'The visual arts, 1603-1740' in T. W. Moody et al. eds. *A New History of Ireland, IV: Eighteenth-Century Ireland,*

1691-1800. Oxford: Clarendon Press.

D'Alton, John (1860). *Illustrations, Historical And Genealogical, of King James's Irish Army List (1689)*. 2nd ed. 2 vols. Dublin: John Falconer.

De la Poer, Count (1898).'The Manor of Kilsheelan'. *Journal of the Waterford and South East of Ireland Archaeological Society*. (4), pp. 116-119.

Dickson, David (1989). 'The Gap in Famines: A Useful Myth' in E. Margaret Crawford ed. *Famine: The Irish Experience 900-1900*. Edinburgh: John Donald Publishers Ltd.

Dickson, David (1997). *Arctic Ireland: The extraordinary story of the Great Frost and Forgotten Famine of 1740-41*. Belfast: The White Row Press.

Dictionary of National Biography (1908-9). 22 vols. Eds. Leslie Stephen and Sidney Lee. London: Smith Elder and Co.

Doubleday, H. A. and Lord Howard de Walden eds. (1911-1940). *The Complete Peerage or a History of the House of Lords and all its Members from the Earliest Times*. 13 vols. London: St Catherine Press.

Dunboyne, Lord (1991). *Butler Family History*. 7th ed. N.p.

Duncan-Jones, Katherine (1991). *Sir Philip Sidney, Courtier Poet*. New Haven & London: Yale University Press.

Empey, C. A. (1970). 'The Butler Lordship in Ireland, 1185-1515'. Unpublished PhD thesis, Trinity College, Dublin.

Empey, C. A. (1985). 'The Norman period, 1185-1500' in William Nolan, ed. *Tipperary: History and Society. Interdisciplinary Essays on the History of an Irish County*. Dublin: Geography Publications.

Empey, C. A. and Katharine Simms (1975). 'The Ordinaries of the White Earl and the Problem of Coign in the later Middle Ages'. *Proceedings of the Royal Irish Academy*. Vol. 75. Section C. No. 8., 161-187.

Gallwey, Hubert (1970). *The Wall Family in Ireland, 1170-1970*. Naas: The Leinster Leader.

Gleeson, Dermot F. (1938). *The Last Lords of Ormond: A History of the 'Countrie of the Three O'Kennedys' during the Seventeenth Century*. London: Sheed & Ward.

Graham, B. J. (1993a). 'Early Medieval Ireland: Settlement, c. 500-1100' in B. J. Graham and L. J. Proudfoot eds. *An Historical Geography of Ireland*. London & San Diego: Academic Press.

Graham, B. J. (1993b). 'The High Middle Ages: c. 1100 to c. 1350' in B. J. Graham and L. J. Proudfoot eds. *An Historical Geography of Ireland*. London & San Diego: Academic Press.

Gwynn, Aubrey & R. Neville Hadcock (1970). *Medieval Religious Houses: Ireland*. London: Longman.

Hae, Risteárd de ed. (1939). *Clár Litridheacht na Nua-Ghaedhilge*. Vol. 2. Dublin: Oifig dhíolta foillseacháin rialtais.

Hennessey, Mark (1985). 'Parochial organisation in medieval Tipperary' in William Nolan, ed. *Tipperary: History and Society. Interdisciplinary Essays on the History of an Irish County.* Dublin: Geography Publications.

Hennessey, Mark (1988). 'The Priory and the Hospital of New Gate: The Evolution and Decline of a Medieval Estate' in William J. Smyth & Kevin Whelan eds. *Common Ground: Essays on the Historical Geography of Ireland.* Cork: Cork University Press.

Hogan, Ed. (1910). *Onomasticon Goedelicum: Locorum et Tribum Hiberniae et Scotiae.* Dublin: Hodges & Figgis & Co. London: Williams & Norgate.

Kelly, James (1995). *'That Damn'd Thing Called Honour': Duelling in Ireland 1570-1860.* Cork: Cork University Press.

Kerrigan, Paul M. (1995). *Castles & Fortifications in Ireland, 1485-1945.* Cork: Collins Press.

Lanigan, Katherine M. (1985). 'Kilcash and the Butlers'. *Journal of the Butler Society.* (2:4) pp. 392-97

Leask, Harold G. (1951). *Irish Castles and Castellated Houses.* Dundalk: Dundalgan Press.

Leask, Harold G. (1977). *Irish Churches and Monastic Buildings: The First Phases and the Romanesque.* Vol. 1. Dundalk: Dundalgan Press.

Little, S. P. (1982). 'Relic of the True Cross'. *Journal of the Butler Society.* Vol. 2, no. 2. P. 193.

Longfield, A. K. (1954). 'Some 18th Century Irish Tombstones'. *The Journal of the Royal Society of Antiquaries of Ireland.* (84:2) pp. 173-9.

Lynch, P. (1815). 'Historical Notices of the Author's Family and Life' in P. Lynch ed. *The Earl of Castlehaven's Memoirs; or, his Review of the Civil Wars in Ireland.* Dublin: Espy and Cross.

Lyons, Monsignor (1937). 'Footprints of Blessed Oliver' in *Blessed Oliver Plunkett Historical Studies.* Dublin: M. H. Gill and Son Ltd.

Maher, James (1954). 'Sacred Relics at Kilcash' in James Maher ed. *Romantic Slievenamon in History, Folklore and Song.* Mullinahone: n.p.

Maher, James (1969). 'The Butlers of Kilcash'. *Old Kilkenny Review.* (21) pp. 83-4.

Maher, James ed. (1954). *Romantic Slievenamon in History, Folklore and Song.* Mullinahone: n.p.

Malins, Edward & The Knight of Glin (1976). *Lost Demesnes: Irish Landscape Gardening, 1660-1845.* London: Barrie & Jenkins Ltd.

Manning, Con (1995). *Early Irish Monasteries.* Dublin: Country House, 1995.

McCarthy, J. F. (1954). 'The Glory of Kilcash: The Gateway to

Slievenamon' in James Maher ed. *Romantic Slievenamon in History, Folklore and Song*. Mullinahone: n.p.

McClintock, Aileen (1988). 'The Earls of Ormond and Tipperary's Role in the Governing of Ireland (1603-1641)'. *Tipperary Historical Journal*. pp. 159-172.

McCracken, J. L. (1986). 'The social structure and social Life, 1714-60' in T. W. Moody et al. eds. *A New History of Ireland, IV: Eighteenth-Century Ireland, 1691-1800*. Oxford: Clarendon Press.

McKeith, Niall E. ed. (1995). *St Patrick's College Maynooth Museum of Ecclesiology: A catalogue of Ecclesiastical items spanning two centuries of the history of the College*. Naas: St Patrick's College, Maynooth.

McLaren, Moray (1972). *Bonnie Prince Charlie*. London: Rupert Hart-Davis.

McNeill, Tom (1997). *Castles in Ireland: Feudal Power in a Gaelic World*. London and New York: Routledge.

Morris, Thomas (1955). 'The Butler Archbishops of Cashel'. *North Munster Antiquarian Journal*. (7:2), pp. 1-11.

Neary, Anne (1984). 'Richard Ledrede: English Franciscan and Bishop of Ossory 1317-c.1360'. *Journal of the Butler Society* (2:3), pp. 273-282.

Neely, W. G. (1989). *Kilkenny: An Urban History, 1391-1843*. Belfast: Institute of Irish Studies.

Nolan, William ed. (1985). *Tipperary: History and Society. Interdisciplinary Essays on the History of an Irish County*. Dublin: Geography Publications.

Ó Cearbhaill, Pádraig (1993). 'Cill Chaise Nó Cill Chais? Logainm í gContae Tiobraíd Árann'. *Éigse: A Journal of Irish Studies* (27), pp. 89-97.

Ó Cuiv, Brian (1986). 'Irish language and literature, 1691-1745' in T. W. Moody et al. eds. *A New History of Ireland, IV: Eighteenth-Century Ireland, 1691-1800*. Oxford: Clarendon Press.

Ó Néill, Eoghan (1988). *Gleann an Óir*. Dublin: Clóchomhar.

O'Donnell, Thomas J. (1960). 'Introduction' to Thomas J. O'Donnell ed. *Selections from the Zeilomastix of Philip O'Sullivan Beare*. Dublin: Stationery Office.

O'Farrell, Fergus (1983). 'Passion Symbols in Irish Church Carvings'. *Old Kilkenny Review*. 2nd Series (2:5), pp. 535-39.

O'Keeffe, Diarmuid (1998). '18th century decorated gravestones: the Kilsheelan-Kilmurry group'. *Tipperary Historical Journal*. pp. 198-214.

Petrie, Charles (1953). *The Marshal Duke of Berwick: The Picture of an Age*. London: Eyre & Spottiswoode.

Petrie, Charles (1975). 'Patrick Sarsfield's Stepson'. *The Irish Sword* (12:47), pp. 153-4.

Pittock, Murray G. H. (1994). *Poetry and Jacobite Politics in Eighteenth-Century Britain and Ireland.* Cambridge: Cambridge University Press.

Power, P. (1952). *The Place-Names of Decies.* 2nd ed. Cork: Cork University Press.

Power, Patrick (1912). *Parochial History of Waterford and Lismore During the 18th and 19th Centuries.* Waterford: N. Harvey & Co.

Power, Patrick (1937). *Waterford and Lismore: A Compendious History of the United Dioceses.* Dublin and Cork: Cork University Press.

Power, Patrick C. (1976). *Carrick-on-Suir and its people.* Dun Laoghaire: The Carrick Society and Anna Livia Books.

Power, Patrick C. (1989). *History of South Tipperary.* Cork and Dublin: The Mercier Press.

Power, Thomas P. (1990). 'Converts' in T. P. Power and Kevin Whelan eds. *Endurance and Emergence: Catholics in Ireland in the Eighteenth Century.* Dublin: Irish Academic Press.

Proudfoot, L. J. (1993). 'Religious Change and Social Protest, c. 1700 to c. 1900' in B. J. Graham and L. J. Proudfoot eds. *An Historical Geography of Ireland.* London & San Diego: Academic Press.

Renehan, Laurence F. (1861). *Collections on Irish Church History.* Ed. Daniel McCarthy. Vol. 1. Dublin: C. M. Warren.

Roe, Helen M. (1983). 'Instruments of the Passion'. *Old Kilkenny Review.* 2nd Series. (2:5) pp. 527-533.

Ryan, James G. (1997). *Irish Records: Sources for Family and Local History.* [USA]: Ancestry Inc.

Salter, Mike (1993). *Castles and Strongholds of Ireland.* Malvern: Folly Publications.

Seymour, St John D. (1989/1913). *Irish Witchcraft and Demonology.* London: Portman Books.

Shearman, John Francis (1879). *Loca Patriciana: An Identification of Localities, Chiefly in Leinster, Visited by Saint Patrick and his Assistant Missionaries.* Dublin: M. H. Gill and Son. London: Burns & Oats.

Silke, John J. (1976). 'The Irish abroad, 1534-1691' in T. W. Moody et al. eds. *A New History of Ireland, III: Early Modern Ireland, 1534-1691.* Oxford: Clarendon Press.

Simms, J. G. (1969). *Jacobite Ireland 1685-91. Studies in Irish History, 2nd series Vol. V.* London: Routledge and Keegan Paul.

Simms, J. G. (1986). 'The Irish on the Continent, 1691-1800' in T. W. Moody et al. eds. *A New History of Ireland, IV: Eighteenth-Century Ireland, 1691-1800.* Oxford: Clarendon Press.

Smyth, William (1985). 'Property, patronage and population: reconstructing the human geography of mid-seventeenth century Tipperary' in William Nolan, ed. *Tipperary: History and Society. Interdisciplinary Essays on the History of an Irish County.* Dublin: Geography Publications.

Sweetman, P. D. (1984). 'Archaeological Excavations at Kilcash Church, Co. Tipperary'. *North Munster Antiquarian Journal.* (26) pp. 36-43.

Thomas, Keith (1991). *Religion and the Decline of Magic: Studies in Popular Belief in Sixteenth- and Seventeenth-Century England.* 2nd ed. London: Penguin Books.

Tone, William Theobald Wolfe (1826). *Life of Theobald Wolfe Tone.* 2 vols. Washington: Gales & Seaton.

Treadwell, Victor (1998). *Buckingham and Ireland 1616-1628: A Study in Anglo-Irish Politics.* Dublin: Four Courts Press.

Wall, Maureen (1989). *Catholic Ireland in the Eighteenth Century: Collected Essays of Maureen Wall.* Ed. Gerard O'Brien. Dublin: Geography Publications.

Williams, Bernadette (1999). '"She was usually placed with the great men and leaders of the land in the public assemblies" – Alice Kyteler: a woman of considerable power' in Christine Meek ed. *Women in Late Medieval and Early Modern Europe.* Dublin: Four Courts Press.

Younger, Carlton (1970). *Ireland's Civil War.* London: Fontana.